GOSPEL
OF VICTORY

GLORIA RUSSELL

authorHOUSE®

AuthorHouse™
1663 Liberty Drive
Bloomington, IN 47403
www.authorhouse.com
Phone: 833-262-8899

Published by AuthorHouse 09/06/2022

ISBN: 978-1-6655-6906-4 (sc)
ISBN: 978-1-6655-6907-1 (e)

Print information available on the last page.

Scripture quotations marked NKJV are taken from the New King James Version. Copyright © 1982 by Thomas Nelson, Inc. Used by permission. All rights reserved.

Scripture quotations marked TPT are from The Passion Translation®. Copyright © 2017, 2018 by Passion & Fire Ministries, Inc. Used by permission. All rights reserved. ThePassionTranslation.com.

This book is printed on acid-free paper.

FOREWORD

The world is ready for some good news! We've come through a storm of negative stuff and we're beginning to see the light at the end of the tunnel. It is critically important that we understand this light. At first glance you may imagine it is an oncoming train. Think again, dear believer.

This light is Jesus Christ, the true Light of the world. Let faith arise. Our God has not forsaken us. He is for us and not against us. Believe again! Everything Jesus accomplished was for His family of believers to live victoriously today and to be eternally with Him in glory. We can make it. Everything we need for a life of victory in Jesus has already been given. This is the gospel of victory!

"But thanks be to God who gives us the victory through our Lord Jesus Christ."

1 Corinthians 15:57

CONTENTS

"But thanks be to God, who gives us the victory through our Lord Jesus Christ."

1 Corinthians 15:57

CHAPTER 1

VICTORY – WHAT IS IT?

Many who know me are aware one of my favorite words is victory. Victory! Say it. "Victory!" Even the sound of the word changes the atmosphere around you. Victory is a shoutin' word – all caps! You can't whisper it. VICTORY! See what I mean?

So what is victory, exactly? In a word – WIN! It's the winning spirit most of us grew up with. We play ball to win; we play chess to win; we compete in a contest of any kind to win; we study to win; we fight to win. Americans have believed and sacrificed long and hard for victory.

My first introduction to the word victory was before Elementary School, going to High School basketball games and yelling my heart out with the cheerleaders. "Victory, victory! That's our cry. V-I-C-T-O-R-Y! Are we in it? Well I guess. Victory, victory, Yes! Yes! Yes!" Never underestimate early childhood experiences!

Victory is the word we use for winning in the world we live in, but more important it is a powerful word in the Kingdom of God. We're not talking about a game or sports competition of some kind. We're talking about life itself. Jesus said, "I have come that you might have life – more abundantly." In this scripture in John 10:10, Jesus compares life without Christ to the life He gives.

In the present season, if you look at world conditions from a human standpoint you will miss what God is saying to His church. Today victory is being proclaimed from almost every church house throughout America. We were created for victory today. The enemy doesn't want you to know this. He's making all kinds of noise to distract believers from a powerful truth that can change your life. If you have received Jesus as your Savior, you are a winner. You can't lose. In every area of your life victory is possible through Jesus Christ who loves you and gave. His life-blood as the price for your sin. Three of the most powerful words ever spoken were said on the cross when Jesus declared, "It is finished!"

Paul must have been thinking of this when he taught 1Corinthians 9:24-27. He uses sporting events to illustrate the winning spirit, saying that a serious athlete will be disciplined in all areas of his life in order to be victorious. This is for a gold medal or watch or belt buckle, but we who follow Jesus Christ live our lives to win a prize that will last forever.

While watching basketball play-offs I discovered something I had not considered before. There were no losers. When you work that hard to get into the play-offs you're already a winner. That's a prize in itself. Similarly, in the Christian life there are no losers. In Christ each and every believer stands victorious. That's what Paul is saying in I Corinthians 15:57.

"Thanks be to God who gives us the victory through our Lord Jesus Christ."

One of the most memorable pictures of victory can be seen in old archives of the day known as V Day, during WWII. (The meaning is obvious). There is a parade down 5th Avenue, in New York City to celebrate the end of the war in Europe with singing, dancing, joyful laughter and tears; flags waving, confetti falling and everyone in America was represented in some way. Men and women still in uniform from all branches of the military marched alongside marching bands, boy scouts, doctors, nurses, construction workers and shop keepers. Everyone was having a party. This unforgettable scene was shown on news reels in every theatre around the world, along with newspaper headlines and magazines declaring victory.

If this in some small way pictures victory in this world, what does a victory celebration look like from heaven's perspective?

Let's consider two possibilities. In Luke 15, Jesus gave three stories to illustrate God's love and concern for people: the parable of the lost sheep; the lost coin, and the lost son. He said two times, "I say to you…there will be more joy in heaven over one sinner who repents…I say to you, there is joy in the presence of the angels of God over one sinner who repents." Of the lost son, the father said, "Bring the fatted calf here and kill it, and let us eat and be merry, for this my son was dead and is alive again; he was lost and is found. And they began to be merry."

What do you think the victory celebration looks like that is taking place in heaven every time anyone receives Christ as Savior or when a back-slider turns back to God? Can you see it? All the angels rejoice. The departed saints rejoice.

Jesus Himself rejoices. There must be a perpetual party going on, on the streets of gold. This is truly V Day from heaven's perspective.

I'm attempting to share the gospel of victory. I have never heard this term used before but I'm beginning to understand when we talk about victory it's always good news. The word gospel literally means good news. It's the good news of all God has done for us through Jesus Christ, our Savior, in His death, burial, and resurrection. Please read that sentence again – dare to exaggerate this truth. You cannot! We are guilty of underestimating the power of what Jesus has done.

There's another victory to consider that from God's perspective must be the greatest victory of all. This is when a child of God enters heaven's gates. When you think of all the ways God has provided for each of us to get through the journey of life, well we can only imagine the celebration that we'll experience. One thing's for sure, no ticker tape parade down 5th Ave. can compare. After all, our precious Lord Jesus' greatest goal is to bring God's family home. (John 3:16)

Jesus said He is preparing a place for us so we can be with Him. (John 14:2) Imagine that…He wants you to be with Him. As long as we are here we can only see and know a few of the things God has planned. Paul wrote 2 Corinthians 5:6-8. Now that will be V Day!

"So we are always confident, knowing that while we are at home in the body we are absent from the Lord. For we walk by faith, not by sight. We are confident, yes, well pleased rather to be absent from the body and to be present with the Lord."

Are we just sitting around waiting for future victories? No, and again I repeat, absolutely not. Today our faith is getting stronger and stronger – from faith to faith. We have victory every time we pray, always praying from victory and not for victory; we find victory in the Word of God, filling us with joy and peace in believing; we experience victory each time we receive one of the precious promises given to help us become more like the Master; we have learned the power of the blood of Jesus Christ to keep on cleansing, restoring, and empowering us to live every day surrounded by Almighty God; victory is being worked out in our lives as we recognize the importance of what we say every day; our worldview is soundly centered in truth and submitted to God's perfect will for a life of victory; we now walk the talk, being doers and not hearers only.

Yes, this very day we declare once again, we have the victory through our Lord Jesus Christ.

"Thanks be to God who gives us the victory through our Lord Jesus Christ.

1 Corinthians 15:57

CHAPTER 2
VICTORY THROUGH FAITH

One of the little decorating fads that seem to have caught on is the use of the word "believe". Perhaps this began when Polar Express first hit the box office. Tom Hanks clicked away on each train ticket to spell out believe. The idea is if you set your mind on something hard enough it becomes your reality. In this case it was to believe in Santa Claus and the North Pole. In one scene a boy whispered, "I believe! I believe! I believe!" We certainly did not need help in the confusing world of fairy tales, but there it is. I'm sure most parents have struggled with what to say when their kids begin to realize they've been taught a lie and how to help them distinguish between truth and fiction/real and pretend.

Believe is a good word as far as it goes. The problem is still believing in the wrong things – lies and deception that keep you from truth. Some think it doesn't matter what you believe in as long as you believe in something. Faith is to believe God is who He says He is and that He will do what He says He will do in His Word. It is confidence in the Person and promises of God. The act of faith is not as important as the object of faith. True faith always leads to the commitment of your life into God's keeping. Faith, like love is demonstrated by obedience. This is true faith and the only path to victory.

What do we mean when we say, "faith alone"? That little statement turned the world upside down in Martin Luther's day. Is it a true statement? Absolutely! The problem is still a total misunderstanding of faith.

One group will say faith plus baptism = salvation; another, faith plus membership in the right church = salvation; then, some add faith plus special requirements = salvation, such as which Bible translation you must use, what day of the week you have church, how much money you should give. On and on it goes where it stops we already know – division/separation. You may get the idea there is a very clever and powerful enemy at work here.

What is the solution? Wars have been fought over this question. Do you still say faith alone =

salvation? Absolutely! How can you say that? The answer is in a correct understanding of faith. Our Heavenly Father does not want any of us to be in the dark on this issue. That's why He wrote so much about it so we can understand. It is possible to say you have faith in God and to live every day as though there is no God. That should not be! When this is the case there are at least two possibilities: you are not born again or you are in great danger of missing God's plan for your life. I encourage you to take care of this today.

The theme of the Gospel of John is believe. John recorded many of his personal experiences of walking with Jesus – miracles he witnessed and in verse 20:31 he tells us the purpose for his writing the book bearing his name.

"These are written that you may believe that Jesus is the Christ, the Son of God, and that believing you may have life in His name."

This is very specific. You must believe in Jesus to have life, both today and for eternity.

The World – Your Enemy

In another book written by John, 1 John 5:4, we find another great truth about faith.

"For whatever is born of God overcomes the world. And this is the victory that has overcome the world, our faith."

Here we've added another dimension to victory – faith to overcome the world. This word "world" means the world system opposing God and under the power of satan. Faith produces life to overcome. Another translation says 1 John 5:4, 5 like this.

"You see every child of God overcomes the world, for our faith is the victorious power that triumphs over the world. So who are the world conquerors, defeating its power? Those who believe that Jesus is the Son of God." 1 John 5:4-5

These scriptures are very revealing to anyone

who desires to live a victorious life. First, it reminds us there is a world system that needs to be defeated. The enemy has very subtlely planted his deceptive evil ideas into the world system we live in. These are in direct opposition to God's ways. You don't have to look far to discover the work of the enemy in this ever-changing world. For example, who would have believed by the 21st Century the majority of Americans are in agreement with abortion rights for women? The result of this great deception is justification to murder thousands of babies each year.

The Devil – Your Enemy

Ephesians 6:16 calls faith a shield to protect us from attacks of the enemy. When you believe in Jesus and receive Him as personal Savior this saving faith is a permanent protection paid for by the blood of Jesus and given as a free gift of salvation. All sin is gone. The enemy no longer has a permanent hold on one who believes in Jesus. You are safely placed into Christ and nothing can take away this relationship.

The Flesh – Your Enemy

There's yet another enemy to deal with – our flesh. Faith can never be taken for granted. On this journey called life there will always be the temptation to give up. To maintain an active, strong faith each day through thick and thin; good times and bad you will need endurance (steadfast courage to keep going with God regardless of what happens). Jesus said he who endures to the end shall be saved. (Matthew 24:13)

God used my friend, Cecil to bring home this truth. Cecil was in a wheel chair and on oxygen for many years before he went home to be with the Lord. His wife faithfully drove him to church three times each week in a special van. One day I asked Cecil what prayer he prayed most often. Without hesitation he answered, "I pray I will not lose my faith." This really puzzled me. How could a man of God who demonstrated strong faith for so many years think he could lose his faith? I'm sure Cecil learned as we all do just how weak the flesh really is. He didn't mean he was fearful of losing his salvation. He was aware a believer must be intentional about growing in faith. Every true follower of Christ desires to finish stronger than we started. Sometimes in the midnight hour, struggling to breath can test the greatest faith.

The first four books in the New Testament are called the Gospels: Matthew, Mark, Luke, and John. These men had the privilege of writing the good news of all that God has done for us through the life of Jesus from His birth to His death, burial and resurrection. Learning from the life of the disciples of Jesus we find evidence of little or weak faith along with God's mercy-in- action to bring each one through times of growing in faith.

In Luke 22, we have the record of Jesus telling Peter that He prayed for him that no matter what happened Peter would stay faithful. Knowing that Peter would soon deny knowing Him, Jesus encouraged Peter by telling him that when Peter turned back to Him, he would be restored and would be able to strengthen the faith of others.

Every believer starts from the same place...at the foot of the cross where Jesus died. From there we receive our marching orders.

"Grow in the grace and knowledge of our Lord Jesus Christ." 2 Peter 3:18

Each believer begins like a newborn baby when we are born-again. Peter wrote 1 Peter 2:2. He knew from personal experience what can happen when your faith is weak.

"As newborn babes, desire the pure milk of the word that you may grow thereby."

SALT

Matthew recorded Jesus instructing His followers to be salt and light. (5:13-16)

"You are the salt of the earth."

Faith is like salt. It permeates every part of your life doing its powerful work in each believer to bring complete victory. If you've ever cooked peas without salt you understand the value of salt. You cannot separate faith into a side dish that you take a bite of when you feel like it.

LIGHT

Faith is also like light. Darkness cannot hide when faith steps in. It has to flee. Doubt and unbelief have to go in the presence of faith. Jesus said, "I am the Light of the world." Here in Matthew 5:14, He says,

"You are the light of the world."

Another important observation of faith is that it is extremely personal. There is no corporate faith and you can't get it on the family plan. Each individual will one day stand before God to answer to Him. Peter wrote that we have been given everything we need to live a victorious life through getting to know Jesus Christ. (2 Peter 1:3, 4) In these scriptures we also learn that faith activates the great and precious promises in God's Word. My job and your job is to believe and God will take care of the rest.

"Believe on the Lord Jesus Christ and you will be saved." Acts 16:31

Another miracle John wrote about was the raising of Jesus' friend Lazarus from the dead. (John 11) Jesus arrived on the scene four days after Lazarus had been buried. His sisters, Mary and Martha were still grieving. Martha said, "Lord, if you had been here, my brother would not have died." Jesus answered, "Your brother will rise again."

Martha blurted out, "I know that he will rise again in the resurrection at the last day." In essence she was complaining that nothing could change their circumstances. She could not see beyond her pain. Jesus answered Martha.

"I am the resurrection and the life. He who believes in Me, though he may die, he shall live. And whoever lives and believes in Me shall never die."

Many in the body of Christ are still confused on this issue and for good reason. All our lives you and I have been bombarded with stories of killing, scenes of funeral services and talk of being put six feet under, etc. Recently, I had a sudden revelation that not one single person that has departed this life has ever been put into a grave – not even a coffin. That's what Jesus meant when he said, "Whoever believes in Me shall never die."

The world system has no other explanation for the departure from earth than the grave. In 2 Corinthians 5, Paul explains that when a believer leaves the body he is immediately present with the Lord. You don't stop for a coffin, or a funeral or a burial at sea – nothing even like that. If you are a true believer, a follower of Jesus Christ you will never die. That's the gospel truth.

What about those who do not know the Lord Jesus? They don't wait for a funeral either. Jesus taught in Luke 16, about a beggar named Lazarus and a rich man that died. The beggar believed in God and was immediately carried by angels to heaven. The rich man (unnamed) being an evil man in this life was immediately in a place of eternal torment. This story printed in red is a quote from Jesus Himself.

All victory comes from knowing Jesus Christ. He has become our salvation. He is our peace. He is our strength for today and hope for tomorrow. He is our ever-present help. He is the light to guide our path. He is the lifter of our head. He is our healer. He is the lover of our soul. He is our friend. The list goes on and on and it's the Gospel of Victory – right from the mouth of God, Himself. What is your need today? He is the Great I AM!

"Thanks be to God who gives us the victory through our Lord Jesus Christ."

1 Corinthians 15:57

CHAPTER 3

VICTORY IN THE SECRET PLACE

Psalm 91

When reading and meditating on the Psalms, as with all scripture we need to remember the Author is Holy Spirit. Therefore, the rich truth we discover becomes personal and applies to every believer today. We can pray the words back to our Father because we have the confident assurance it is in His will. Faith grows and God is pleased.

In Psalm 91, we are immediately invited into the presence of God and reminded of how the Word works in our lives. Let's read it again, as if it is the first time.

"He who dwells in the secret place of the Most High shall abide under the shadow of the Almighty. I will say of the Lord, "He is my refuge and

my fortress; My God in Him I will trust. Surely He shall deliver you from the snare of the fowler and from the perilous pestilence. He shall cover you with His feathers, and under His wings you shall take refuge; His truth shall be your shield and buckler. You shall not be afraid of the terror by night, nor of the arrow that flies by day, nor of the pestilence that walks in darkness, nor of the destruction that lays waste at noonday. A thousand may fall at your side, and ten thousand at your right hand; but it shall not come near you. Only with your eyes shall you look and see the reward of the wicked. Because you have made the Lord, who is my refuge, even the Most High your dwelling place, no evil shall befall you, nor shall any plague come near your *dwelling; For He shall give His angels charge over you, to keep you in all your ways. In their hands they shall bear you up, lest you dash your foot against a stone. You shall tread upon the lion and the cobra, the young lion and the serpent you shall trample underfoot. Because he has set his love upon Me, therefore I will deliver him; I will set him on high, because he has known My name. He shall call upon Me, and I will answer him; I will be with him in trouble; I will deliver him and honor him. With long life I will satisfy him, and show him My salvation." Psalm 91*

When one lives in constant communion with God he is forever safe in God's protective care. This is God's secret place of prayer and we are invited to stay there safe and secure at all times. Prayer is simply talking to the One who loves you and the One you love the most. It is a relationship that is most precious and permanent. One we can always count on.

1 Thessalonians 5:17 instructs us to "pray without ceasing". This is more than an attitude – it is a Presence. It is the abiding presence of our Lord, His fellowship, His comfort, His encouragement, His protection.

Matthew 6:6 "But you, when you pray, go into your room, and when you have shut the door pray to your Father who is in the secret place, and your Father who sees in secret will reward you openly."

The word dwelling in Psalm 91:1, implies being at home in God – loving His presence. It is our privilege to live under His protection, surrounded as a dot within a circle as God's own special child, without fear. (Titus 2:14) This covenant circle is our dwelling place. Nothing can harm us or take us out of His hands as He promised.

In Psalm 91:1, 2 there are four titles for God

to help us understand who God is and how He relates to our lives.

- Elyon reveals to us that God is the "Highest". He is the Most High, worthy to receive glory and honor and power and is to be worshiped forever. In verse 1, Most High is Elyon. His right to rule over us is absolute. We must guard against rebellion in our lives. Self-rule is one of the most dangerous sins of the flesh. This independent spirit resists authority and refuses to be ruled by God. It may feel like victory to your flesh but there is no freedom—no victory outside of God's protective covering. (v.1)

- Shaddai, (verse 1) is the name God revealed Himself to Abraham, Isaac, and Jacob, meaning Almighty, the "All Sufficient Mighty One", God who is more than enough; the One who gives strength and satisfies every need we have; a God of might and miracles.

- Jehovah (Yahweh) is the most frequently used name in the Bible. In verse 2,"Lord" is Jehovah. Through this name Holy Spirit reveals to us a God who is absolutely self-existent and holy above all else. Jehovah hates sin and loves righteousness. (Ps. 11:9) He is grieved when His people turn away from Him.

- Elohim is "my God" in verse 2. This is the first name the Lord used to describe Himself. Elohim is a plural noun revealing from the beginning God as a trinity: Father, Son, and Holy Spirit, the only true and living God. Elohim created us by His power and put Himself in a covenant relationship with man through the blood of His covenant.

Indulge me as I share Gloria's amplified translation. A believer, who is at home in the secret place of Elyon, the Most High God, awesome in majesty, shall continue in unbroken fellowship under the shadow of Shaddai, the Almighty all-sufficient God. I will say of Jehovah, my LORD, the Holy One who loves the righteousness only He can give, He is my shelter from danger; my place of protection; my Elohim: God the Father, God the Son, and God the Holy Spirit, who I trust.

Psalm 91, cannot be fully appreciated without the understanding of a metaphor, which is a figure of speech referring to one thing by mentioning another, suggesting similarity. Example: 1 Peter 5:8.

"The devil walks about like a roaring lion, seeking whom he may devour."

Peter is giving a warning about the devil, by mentioning a roaring lion, meaning the devil walks or roams about like a lion. The devil is not a lion, but this suggests similarity between a lion and the devil. When lions hunt, they look for weak, young, isolated, unguarded animals. They are the ones marked for attack. This helps us to understand the devil is like that. It is dangerous to live your life in isolation. We need the body of Christ.

Beginning with verse 2, "He is my fortress" takes us to a fort or armed embassy where one can find a place of safety. The Psalmist mentions this as being similar or compared to the protection of the LORD, Yahweh. We can always run to Him in times of danger, or when we have missed the mark, and He will protect us and forgive us our sins.

Next, in verse 3, "snare of the fowler" is a great picture of a fowler, who is someone skilled at catching birds. Our God will surely deliver you from a very clever enemy when you are captured or feel you are in a cage. 2 Timothy 2:25, 26 make this clear for today. "…correcting those who are in opposition, if perhaps God will grant them repentance, so that they may know the truth, and that they may come to their senses and escape the snare of the devil, having been taken captive by him to do his will." The Psalmist adds more. God will also deliver you from the "perilous pestilence", referring to an attack that comes like a plague, swift and deadly. We can surely understand God's mighty power of protection from a plague, such as Covid 19, the flu, and all the variants. There are many perilous pestilences today. Knowing the truth sets captives free – those the enemy is using to do his bidding.

Verse 4, the Psalmist directs his instruction to you personally. "He shall cover you with His feathers and under His wings you shall take refuge." He so beautifully pictures our Father's loving protection by using the metaphor of a hen protecting her chickens from birds of prey, fire, or other dangers. The chicks run under her wings at the slightest threat. When I was a child I remember Grandpa helping a little with an old shotgun he kept close for this purpose. Chicken hawks and snakes were a real problem for poor folk who depended on chickens to keep them from starving. Matthew 23:37, records the occasion of our Lord Jesus weeping over Jerusalem saying He wanted to gather them together as a hen gathers her chicks under her wings, but they refused His help. That's the Father's heart. He doesn't want anyone to perish or to be lost, however, you can refuse Him.

Here we learn God is willing to guard His people as a hen guards the chickens and He is as able as a man of war in full armor. "His truth shall be your shield and buckler." Shield and buckler were two Roman shields of different sizes providing complete protection in battle. This metaphor pictures God's truth as being similar. We are just getting a glimpse of the power of God's Word. Truth is in Jesus, the Living Word, and God has given us the written Word to know the Truth that sets us free. The enemy can only lie and deceive. The Spirit of God is reminding us once again that we must pay attention to the word God speaks. We need to mediate, read again and examine meanings carefully. Some of the simplest words that we think we understand can with another look explode with meaning.

A couple of years ago the word God spoke to me for this season is, "Truth matters." Since then we have watched as fake news and fact checks have been added to our vocabulary. As this increases, the enemy is having a field day! Lies and deception could trap us if we do not begin to take seriously the Word of God. What God says is the only truth to protect us completely. It is our sword and shield. (Eph. 6:17)

The Psalmist continues declaring in spite of all danger, great security is promised by having a strong faith-shield. "You shall not be afraid." Overcoming fear is the first step to victorious living. In verses 5 – 8, we see there are circumstances and dangers all around us, "day, night, and noonday." The wicked one works hard to bring us down. However, we have God's direct command to follow: Fear not! Fear not! Fear not!

Fear has torment. God keeps us from all kinds of fear the enemy may use to paralyze us. Jesus

Himself said, "Do not fear those who kill the body but cannot kill the soul."

Fear is defined as a panic that grips a person causing him to run away, be alarmed, scared, frightened, dismayed, filled with dread, intimidated, anxious, and apprehensive. This kind of fear is destructive. Compare this to the reverential awe or fear of God which is constructive, producing wisdom with ability to separate between what is good and what is bad, and have spiritual understanding of the purpose of trials. (Proverbs 9:10; James 1:5)

Proverbs 29:25 addresses both.

"The fear of man brings a snare, but whoever trusts in the LORD shall be secure."

The New Testament upgrades this thought with 2 Timothy 1:7. Being filled with the Spirit of God will cause you to become fearless.

"But God has not given us a spirit of fear but of power and of love and of a sound mind."

Grasping these truths is critical for spiritual maturity. The enemy has demonic angels who feed on fear. These spirits are not from God. They paralyze and torment a believer which causes one to feel powerless and alone. In the face of fear we must learn to run immediately into God's safe keeping.

Here are three things to remember when fear is on the attack.

(1) Acknowledge the power of God who lives in you. Become God inside minded.
(2) Remember the perfect love He has for you.
(3) The mind of Christ to guide you in making wise choices.

Verse 9, "Because you have made the LORD who is my refuge, even the Most High, your dwelling place, no evil shall befall you, nor shall any plague come near your dwelling."

1. The word refuge means a shelter, a place of trust, suggesting to flee for protection, to confide in.

2. Dwelling place indicates a retreat, describing the security of intimately dwelling together, as in marriage.

When we make the Lord our refuge and habitation by trusting Him – taking our cares, fears, and needs to Him; by seeking His counsel, spending times of refreshing with Him; and by loving Him and walking closely with Him every day, we enter into a sheltered place of promise regarding health. These promises do not say we are totally immune from calamities, but we are promised His presence and deliverance when we call upon Him. If you have been a follower of Christ for very long you will easily relate to God's power to heal.

Psalm 91 gives great and precious promises we can count on today. God speaks most directly with promises of protection from sickness and disease for the redeemed. We must remember these promises are conditioned upon making the Lord our true refuge and habitation.

Followers of Jesus Christ have God's Word that we are protected. We are the ones who have made the Most High our habitation. We are in His presence 24/7, experiencing His love, protection, and provision. We walk with Him and talk with Him and depend on Him in the secret place of prayer. We are kept in perfect peace. When you think about it, whatever happens in our lives nothing really hurts us. (v.10)

Verses 11, 12 "For He shall give His angels charge over you to keep you in all your ways. In their hands they shall bear you up lest you dash your foot against a stone." As if we did not have enough protection, God has promised the presence and help of His angels. These ministering angels are on assignment by God and are with you continually, watching out for you in every circumstance. (Matt.4:6)

Verse 13, "You shall tread upon the lion and the cobra, the young lion and the serpent you shall trample underfoot." The Psalmist use of lion, cobra, young lion, and serpent speak of demonic enemies roaming about, seeking to completely destroy the believer. Note the use of "you shall", rather than "if you". I'm sure we would be surprised at how often this scripture is being applied to our lives. The enemy is always on the job and this promise is very personal to each of us. "In Christ" we are the victorious warriors who have authority over the works of the enemy.

You can't read this without being aware we are in a war. The fight of faith is part of the walk. (1 Timothy 6:12)

God is speaking to you who walk daily with Him and He underscores these personal promises signed, sealed, and delivered with, "I will", six times in verses 14 – 16.

Therefore:

1. "I will deliver him". How many rescues have you experienced personally? These are just the ones you are aware of.

2. "I will set him on high" (exalt you). In Christ you are exalted…beloved… anointed king! This means you are already seated with our Lord in the heavenlies – high above the world with all its problems and the effects of its evil.

3. "I will answer him". Read again the great and precious promise that assures us of God hearing and answering prayer. Many times I pray, "Lord, I believe. Help my unbelief." The Holy Spirit is moving us from faith to greater faith.

4. "I will be with him in trouble". He has never failed you yet!

5. "I will deliver him and honor him." He not only delivers you, but honors you. This is almost too hard to grasp. On the other hand, what greater honor could we have than to have Almighty God come to live inside by His Holy Spirit?

6. "I will satisfy him with long life". Each life regardless of length of days is full and complete when our Father calls us home, whether 30 years or 80 years. When we finish the work He assigned for us we certainly would not want to stay here one day longer. "And show him My salvation". We will see Him face to face and all questions will be answered.

2 Corinthians 1:20 gives the New Testament guarantee concerning promises. Remember the definition of "all" is all!

"For all the promises of God in Him are yes, and in Him, amen, to the Glory of God."

Notice who receives these promises in Psalm

91:14. Don't you love the Psalmist use of personal pronouns?

- You set your love on Me.
- You know My name.

Hebrews 13:5, 6 seals the deal:

"...be content with such things as you have. For He Himself has said, I will never leave you nor forsake you. So we may boldly say: The LORD is my helper. I will not fear. What can man do to me?"

It's time to believe God's Word and to experience victory in the secret place.

"But thanks be to God who gives us the victory through our Lord Jesus Christ."

1 Corinthians 15:57

CHAPTER 4

VICTORY THROUGH THE WORD

I have recently been challenged to re-examine one of the core beliefs of the faith. Through this study perhaps we can discover what the Spirit is saying to His church in this season.

Let's plunge in with the question of inspiration of the scriptures by going to the most important statement on this subject recorded in scripture: 2 Timothy 3:16.

All Scripture is given by inspiration of God, and is profitable for:

Doctrine – Sound doctrine is truth found only in God's Word. This is the truth that sets one free. Doctrine is teaching in the Word of God. To have victory in this life it is absolutely essential to know God's Word and the one true God revealed in His Word. My prayer is that God will open our eyes to this truth. Believers have always talked about the Bible far more than to actually read the Bible. There is no shortcut. This is God's plan and the only way our faith can grow.

Reproof – This is God's spotlight shining on areas needing attention where one might have missed it. That just about fits us all!

Correction – The power of God at work through the Word of God to correct an area or problem that we got wrong. One must be willing for correction to happen. When the Holy Spirit shines the spotlight on an area that's the time to repent and let God do the correction needed.

Instruction in righteousness – Training, discipline; being conformed to the revealed will of God in all areas, with God's character being lived out through your life.

Do you see the progression here? First you have doctrine so you can know what God says. The Word reveals sin and you submit to God's correction. Then you begin to grow, grow, grow!

The word inspiration clears up some questions right up front. Inspiration means, "God-breathed." Perhaps we forgot the Author of the entire Word of God is God the Holy Spirit. It is not the product of human intelligence, but is directly "breathed" by God Himself. This biblical view is called the <u>plenary verbal inspiration</u> of Scriptures, meaning every word is inspired by the Holy Spirit of God.

2 Timothy 3:17 "...that the man of God may be complete, thoroughly equipped for every good work."

Consider this from The Passion Translation. "Every Scripture has been inspired by the Holy Spirit, the breath of God. It will empower you by its instruction and correction, giving you the strength to take the right direction and lead you deeper into the path of godliness."

Every man and woman of God can be complete – made whole, and thoroughly equipped for life through the Word of God, knowing Jesus our Savior, and living by the power of God's indwelling Spirit.

Remember 2 Peter 1: 3, 4 says it like this,

"His divine power has given to us all things that pertain to life and godliness through the knowledge of Him who called

us by glory and virtue by which have been given to us exceedingly great and precious promises that through these you may be partakers of the divine nature having escaped the corruption that is in the world through lust."

The absolute authority of the Bible over our lives is based on our conviction that this book does not merely contain the Word of God, but that it is the Word of God, beginning in Genesis 1:1, all the way to Revelation 22:21.

Let's take a closer look.

"Knowing first that no prophesy of Scripture is of any private interpretation (or origin), for prophecy never came by the will of man, but holy men of God spoke as they were moved by the Holy Spirit." 2 Peter 1:20, 21

"Now we have received, not the spirit of the world, but the Spirit who is from God, that we might know the things that have been freely given to us by God. These things we also speak, not in words which man's wisdom teaches but which the Holy Spirit teaches, comparing spiritual things with spiritual." 1 Corinthians 2:12-15

The Holy Spirit is not only the Author of the Word; He is the Teacher – your personal tutor.

This is not to say the writers of Scripture were like robots being used to write automatically. Each writer involved in the production of the Holy Scriptures was "moved" (literally, being borne along) by the Holy Spirit. Even the words used, (the precise terminology) were planned by the Spirit of God and given to the various writers. Jesus Himself confirmed this truth by saying,

"For I say to you, until heaven and earth pass away, one jot or one tittle

shall in no wise pass from the law, until all be fulfilled."

Why is this important? 2 Timothy 3:13, 14 give this explanation.

"But evil men and imposters will grow worse and worse, deceiving and being deceived. But you must continue in the things you have learned and been assured of, knowing from whom you have learned them."

As we have seen, the Bible has a lot to say about itself. In this study I want to look at several important facts recorded for the body of Christ so we can know the truth about God's Word. At first glance this may seem elementary but believe me when I say we live in times of great deception and we must know what we believe, remember it, and meditate on it lest we fall prey to the enemies of God's Word.

2 Samuel 22:31, is my latest find. (Sometimes

I feel like I'm searching for precious stones.) This one is a jewel!

"As for God His way is perfect. The word of the LORD is proven (flawless). He is a shield to all who trust in Him."

Flawless means proven to have no defect, fault, or error. I cannot understand anyone who thinks our God would give us His Word filled with error, contradictions, or out and out lies. Do I have a closed mind? Yes indeed! I won't even entertain the possibility. You see, I know the Author, personally. If human beings like myself were the author – but then, we've already settled that, haven't we?

Another scripture that reveals the complete trustworthiness of the Holy Scriptures which constitute the Bible is found in one of David's Psalms. Psalm 19:7-11.

"The law of the LORD is perfect, converting (restoring) the soul. The testimony of the LORD is sure, making

wise the simple; the statues of the LORD are right, rejoicing the heart; the commandment of the LORD is pure, enlightening the eyes; the fear of the LORD is clean, enduring forever; the judgments of the LORD are true and righteous altogether. More to be desired are they than gold, yea, than much fine gold; sweeter also than honey and the honeycomb. Moreover by them your servant is warned, and in keeping them there is great reward."

Perfect, sure, right, pure, enlightening, clean, true, righteous, sweet! These are words that would be pretty hard to misinterpret. They speak of characteristics of the Bible. There are two terms we use to describe these features of God's Word.

1. Inerrant (perfect) means that in the original writings of each book included in the 66 books there was no mistakes or error of any kind.

2. <u>Infallible</u> refers to the absolute trustworthiness of the Bible to guide our belief in God and our life as a believer.

There's another point that needs to be made here. Many question whether we can trust the copies of Scriptures we have today. This too has been guided by the Holy Spirit over the centuries so we have the same inerrant, infallible Word we can trust.

What should be our response to the truth in God's Word? I found a great example in Ezra 7:10 which tell us this man of God, Ezra, both studied, as he sought the Lord and obeyed what he learned in the law of the LORD.

Compare Psalm 19:7.

"The law of the LORD is perfect, converting or restoring the soul."

David also wrote in the 23rd Psalm, verse 3,

"He restores my soul."

Add Paul's testimony in 2 Corinthians 4:16.

"...the inward man is being renewed day by day."

These examples teach us the converting, restoring, renewing power of the Word of God. In Ezra 7:10, we read that Ezra prepared his heart to do this. We would be wise to follow his example. I have learned that I have to be intentional about Bible study. Daily restoration of the soul (mind, emotions, will) is critical to well-being. You won't find help for doubt, fear, anxiety, weariness, etc. anywhere else.

How would you prepare your heart for this important project? We might take a clue from Daniel who "purposed in his heart" not to eat the pagan food of the Babylonians which had been offered to their idols. That means he decided, made up his mind in advance. I think this might be the first step to preparing your heart to study and obey the Bible. With the busy lifestyle of today all your best intentions will be thwarted otherwise. You have to do it on purpose as one does any other important appointment. This one just happens to be a life/death issue in your relationship with God.

The writer of Hebrews in 11:6 says,

"Without faith it is impossible to please Him..."

We agree we want to please our Lord so how can we get God-pleasing faith? You remember Romans 10:17—faith comes from the Word of God. No Word = no faith! Little Word = little faith! More Word = more faith! Much Word = great faith! It really is that simple.

Last but not least let's turn to Psalm 119. This is perhaps the most important book in the Bible concerning its superiority. David uses seven words to refer to the Word of God: law, commandments, testimonies, statues, precepts, judgments, and ordinances to declare the multi-faceted, revealed will of God. In this Psalm we have David's prayer and life testimony that God's Word is truth that endures forever. He said this in verse 160.

"The entrance of Your word is truth..."

When any believer decides to actually follow Jesus, obeying what His Word teaches, you will take steps toward aligning with truth. Not just anything the world considers truth, but the only real truth, which is Jesus who said,

"I am the way, the truth, and the life..." John 14:6

David's prayers recorded in Psalm 119, are excellent examples of how to pray. David aligned himself with God's Word, God's will, and God's ways. That should be the desire of every believer today. It would be good to remember why these truths are still applicable. The Author, the Holy Spirit of God has given us a guide to get us on the right path and His abiding presence to keep us there.

In verse 126, David pleads with God to act because "they have regarded Your law as void." What happens if you write a check to one of your creditors, then mark it void? It is cancelled, right? It cannot be taken from your account balance.

It seems there are those who claim to be believers who also want to cancel the Old Testament altogether. They have marked it void – cancelled. Sorry! You can't do that. God's Word is firmly settled in heaven. (v. 89)

Peter wrote in 2 Peter 1:19

"And so we have the prophetic word confirmed (message from the prophets), which you do well to heed as a light that shines in a dark place..."

He clearly believed the Old Testament to be equally inspired and useful to guide us.

Here is a brief overview of Psalm 119, concerning the value of God's Word in its entirety:

- The way to happiness – Verse 1 sets the theme of this song revealing the key to happiness (blessed) is doing what God says in His Word.
- The Word has cleansing power when we apply ourselves to learn from it and to receive counsel from it. Isaiah called Jesus, Wonderful Counselor.
- Hope comes from the Word as we get to know our God. His Word is always faithful. You can expect the goodness of God every time.
- God's Word gives life. David says God's Word has no limits!

- Wisdom and understanding come from the Word as the Holy Spirit of God teaches us. Biblical understanding far surpasses the intellect. Daniel 2:21, "He gives wisdom to the wise and knowledge to them that know understanding.

- Psalm 119:105 "Your Word is a lamp to my feet, and a light to my path." Verse 130 teaches "The entrance of Your words gives light. It gives understanding to the simple."

God's Word lights the way before you, giving clear direction for each step (to your feet), as well as wisdom for the journey (to your path). It is foolish to stay in the dark when God's light is available. Jesus made this very clear in John 8:12.

"I am the Light of the world...He who follows Me shall not walk in darkness, but have the light of life."

As you allow God's Word to guide, correct, instruct, lead, teach, and confirm, you need never fear any enemy that comes against you. God becomes a hiding place of safety and a shield to protect you. You have His promise that He will never leave you nor forsake you. (Hebrews 13:5) Great peace is promised to anyone who loves God's Word.

I think we can safely say, victory comes through the Word!

"*Thanks be to God who gives us the victory through our Lord Jesus Christ.*

1 Corinthians 15:57

CHAPTER 5

VICTORY IN THE PRECIOUS PROMISES

Perhaps you've said to someone, "Promises! Promises! Promises!" If yes, you have encountered someone you do not trust to keep his word. Maybe your Dad said, "We'll go to Disneyworld soon." Your response may have been, "You promise?" "Yes, I promise", he replies confidently. You may or may not go to Disneyworld, but it is not unusual for humans to fail to keep promises. We definitely have limitations.

Almighty God is the only true Promise Keeper. His promises are solid and true, based on His trustworthiness and power.

2 Corinthians 1:20 "For all the promises of God in Him are yes, and in Him amen, to the glory of God through us."

In The Passion Translation we read this

scripture. "For all of God's promises find their "yes" of fulfillment in Him. And as His "yes" and our "amen" (meaning "That's right!") ascend to God we bring Him glory." This could imply, it is through Christ that we hear and believe God's promises and say the declaration of our faith, "I agree".

Promises of the Father

Luke 24:49 "Behold, I send the Promise of My Father upon you..."

Jesus was prophesying of the coming of the Holy Spirit on the Day of Pentecost. This was the promise the Father made of enabling power. It is this promise of supernatural power that Jesus uses to fulfill His mission to the world through His Church – the church He is building.

Peter preached about this after Pentecost. This is the promise of the Father.

"Therefore, being exalted to the right hand of God, and having received from

the Father the promise of the Holy Spirit. He poured out this which you now see and hear."

Again, in Acts 2:39.

"For the promise is to you and to your children, and to all who are afar off, as many as the Lord our God will call."

All who are afar off includes Gentiles – you and me. Peter's words clearly extend to every believer the same experience of the first believers who received the Holy Spirit at the birth of the church.

"Therefore, since a promise remains of entering His rest let us fear lest any of you seem to have come short of it."
Hebrews 4:1

The faith-rest in this verse is being free from striving (working), fully surrendered to the Lordship of Christ, and totally controlled by the

Holy Spirit. The full impact of this promised rest is found in Hebrews 10:35, 36.

"Therefore do not cast away your confidence which has great reward. For you have need of endurance so that after you have done the will of God you may receive the promise."

The future consummation of our salvation will not waver because it is grounded on the faithfulness of the One who promised. Add to that Numbers 23:19.

"God is not a man, that He should lie..."

What God has promised, He will do. 1 Peter 2:22 assures us that Jesus never lied or deceived anyone.

Promises of Jesus

Jesus Himself affirmed the Father's promise of Holy Spirit in Acts 1:8.

"But you shall receive power when the Holy Spirit has come upon you and you shall be witnesses to Me..."

Again, from the words of Jesus.

"He who believes in Me, as the Scripture has said, out of his heart will flow rivers of living water."

John explains John 7:39 in verse 39.

"But this He spoke concerning the Spirit whom those believing in Him would receive; for the Holy Spirit was not yet given, because Jesus was not yet glorified."

Promises the Holy Spirit fulfilled

The Holy Spirit not only reminds us of what Jesus taught but He guides us into further truth, giving us an understanding of how the word works in our lives to accomplish God's perfect plan. (This is covered in Chapter 4)

> *John 14:26 "But the Helper (or Comforter) the Holy Spirit, whom the Father will send in My name, He will teach you all things and bring to your remembrance all things that I said to you."*

> *John 16:13 "However, when He the Spirit of truth has come, He will guide you into all truth..."*

> *Romans 8:26 "Likewise the Spirit also helps in our weaknesses. For we do not know what we should pray for as we ought, but the Spirit Himself makes intercession for us with groaning which cannot be uttered."*

When you hear these promises and believe God, faith always releases the power of God's Word. We can count on the Holy Spirit to teach us all things we need to know, guide us to the truth and nothing but the truth, and pray for us the perfect will of God. His promises are true.

I have discovered what must be the clearest explanation of victory in the precious promises. I used this scripture in another chapter, but it is worth repeating and looking a little deeper. This began with an assignment from God to memorize 2 Peter 1:3, 4. (Not the easiest assignment I've received) To accomplish this great feat I began to break it down, analyze word meanings, and meditate on this great promise. It is so powerful and so important to our Christian walk I'd like to share what I have received so you can compare and add to your own understanding.

"His divine power has given to us all things that pertain to life and godliness through the knowledge of Him who called us by glory and virtue, by which have been given to us exceedingly great and

precious promises, that through these you may be partakers of His divine nature, having escaped the corruption that is in the world through lust."

You notice right away this had to be written by the Holy Spirit of God rather than by an uneducated fisherman. It is a declaration of a completed transaction, accomplished when any individual receives Jesus as Savior and Lord. "It's a done deal" some would say!

"His divine power" would be the supernatural Holy Spirit of God who comes to live in the heart at the new birth as a permanent presence of Almighty God. At that time He deposited within you everything you need to live a life of power and godliness. Everything needed to reflect God's true nature has already been given to you – "already been given", past tense. How is it possible to share the divine nature of Jesus and to be a reflection of the true nature of God? Connect the dots! "Greater is He that is in you…" (1 John 4:4) The Greater One lives in you. The promise of the Father confirmed by our Lord Jesus, the mighty Holy Spirit lives in you – greater than any obstacle; greater than any sickness; greater than the limitations of the flesh; greater than any work of the devil; greater than the world system we live in.

Paul wrote in 2 Corinthians 1:20 – 22.

"For all the promises of God in Him are Yes, and in Him, Amen, to the glory of God through us. Now He who establishes us with you in Christ and has anointed us is God, who also has sealed us and given us the Spirit in our hearts as a guarantee."

Notice the entire Godhead is involved. Peter says that everything we receive comes through "the knowledge of Jesus". Knowledge is more than intelligence or simply knowing about God. Knowledge is an intimate term meaning to experience God and Jesus in His transforming power, first hand, up close and personal. Then he says we have been given "exceedingly great and precious promises" in order to share the holy nature of God. Imagine that! Our Heavenly

Father not only loves us and provided salvation for us through the death of His only Son; He also desires to share His very nature with us. Run—don't walk to take advantage of this once in a lifetime offer!

It would be good to remember and reflect on some of the great and precious promises we have been given.

Life for the world we live in:

- Abundant life – Jesus said, "I have come that you may have life…more abundantly." John 10:10
- Love – "This is My commandment, that you love one another as I have loved you." John 13:34
- Forgiveness and cleansing – "If we confess our sins, He is faithful and just to forgive us our sins and to cleanse us from all unrighteousness." 1 John 1:9
- Light – "You are the light of the world… Let your light so shine before men, that they may see your good works and glorify your Father in Heaven." Matthew 5:14a, 16

- Peace – "Peace I leave with you, My peace I give to you…" John 14:27a
- Grace – "But to each one of us grace was given according to the measure of Christ's gift." Ephesians 4:7
- Hope – "And now Lord, what do I wait for? My hope is in You." Psalm 39:7
- Protection – "But whoever listens to Me will dwell safely, and will be secure, without fear of evil." Proverbs 1:33
- Provision – "And my God shall supply all your need according to His riches in glory by Christ Jesus." Philippians 4:19
- Strength – "I can do all things through Christ who strengthens me." Philippians 4:13
- Courage – "Be strong and of good courage, do not fear, nor be afraid of them; for the LORD your God, He is the One who goes with you. He will not leave you nor forsake you." Deuteronomy 31:6
- Joy – "These things I have spoken to you that My joy may remain in you and that your joy may be full." John 15:11

- Power – "For God has not given us a spirit of fear, but of power and of love and of a sound mind." 2 Timothy 1:7

Life in the Kingdom of God:

- Love – "And we have known and believed the love that God has for us. God is love and he who abides in love abides in God and God in him." 1 John 4:16
- Life – "Reckon yourselves to be dead indeed to sin, but alive to God in Christ Jesus our Lord." Romans 6:11
- Light – "…walk as children of light: (for the fruit of the Spirit is in all goodness and righteousness and truth) Proving what is acceptable unto the Lord." Ephesians 5:8b - 10
- Righteousness – "…he who practices righteousness is righteous, just as He is righteous." 1 John 3:7b
- Spiritual senses – "But solid food belongs to those who are of full age, that is, those who by reason of use have their senses exercised to discern both good and evil." Hebrews 5:14

- Peace – "Therefore, having been justified by faith, we have peace with God through our Lord Jesus Christ." Romans 5:1
- Praise – "I will bless the LORD at all times; His praise shall continually be in my mouth." Psalm 34:1
- Hope – "Now may the God of hope fill you with all joy and peace in believing, that you may abound in hope by the power of the Holy Spirit." Romans 15:13
- Worship – "God is Spirit, and those who worship Him must worship in spirit and truth." John 4:24
- Faith – "Above all taking the shield of faith with which you will be able to quench all the fiery darts of the wicked one." Ephesians 6:16
- Answered prayer – "If you abide in Me, and My words abide in you, you will ask what you desire, and it shall be done for you." John 15:7
- Counsel – "I will instruct you and teach you in the way you should go; I will counsel you with My loving eye on you." Psalm 32:8

- Presence of God – "I will not leave you orphans; I will come to you...If anyone loves Me, he will keep My word; and My Father will love him, and We will come to him and make our home with him." John 14:18, 23
- Redemption – "Whoever has been born of God does not sin, for His seed remains in him; and he cannot sin, because he has been born of God." 1 John 3:9

These are just a few of the things God has given to help us live according to His will and purpose. There are two keys you will need:

1. <u>Get to know Jesus more and more.</u>
   Everything we receive from God comes from our knowing Jesus.

"Grow in His grace and kindness knowing He loves you." 2 Peter 3:18.

As you focus on Jesus as Lord (boss) of your life you have literally hundreds, maybe thousands of precious promises available that you may share a deep spiritual union with Christ Jesus. Understand that all of this is provided simply because you know Him.

2. <u>Receive all that God has provided.</u>
   This could be the missing link. You must move from head knowledge to a work of God deep in your heart. Believe! Beginning with John 3:16, from there the resources available to a believer are endless.

"He who did not spare His own Son, but delivered Him up for us all; how shall He not with Him also freely give us all things?" Romans 8:32

Why would anyone not want to receive all that God has provided? Unbelief perhaps. Our minds tell us it's too good to be true, or I don't deserve it, or there's no such thing as more. This is like saying to a growing child, "OK, you have all you need. This is it! There is no more."

Begin to rehearse the promises over in your mind. Write and display them where you can read regularly. Ask Holy Spirit which promise to begin with and take them one at a time. Example: Righteousness.

> *"...he who practices righteousness is righteous, as He is righteous."*
> *1 John 3:7b.*

Begin repeating, "I am the righteousness of God in Christ Jesus." This method will build your faith since faith comes by the Word of God. Your part is to believe it!

How many precious promises do you know and believe God for?

"Thanks be to God who gives us the victory through our Lord Jesus Christ."

1 Corinthians 15:57

CHAPTER 6

VICTORY IN THE BLOOD

"The blood of Jesus Christ, God's Son (continually) cleanses us from all sin."
1 John 1:7

Once in travail over a lost loved one who seemed beyond help, I heard in my spirit, "The blood is enough!" The issue was settled. God had spoken and I was at peace. Since then, I have learned to listen, meditate, and trust the Holy Spirit's little one-liners. They are always packed with truth for a life-time. This is what Jesus was saying in Matthew 4:46.

"It is written, man shall not live by bread alone but by every word that proceeds from the mouth of God."

God is always talking. The problem is in our ability to hear. Spiritual senses are developed as we continue to walk with God and by faith learn to exercise these senses. Jesus also said,

"My sheep hear My voice and I know them and they follow Me." John 10:27

Our first understanding of the importance of the blood comes when we hear the gospel message that teaches God the Son, Jesus Christ through whom the worlds were created became flesh (was born), grew to be a man, and died on the cross for our sins, was buried and came to life again. (1 Corinthians 15:3, 4) This plan of redemption was in the heart of Almighty God (Father, Son, and Holy Spirit) before creation. (See 1 Peter 1:20) We often forget just how involved God is with our lives. Every detail of God's plan to populate heaven was worked out and is being executed, even today in your life and my life. Most of us can testify of the great lengths God went to reach us while we were still in unbelief, and an even greater effort has kept us safe on the journey.

We have the privilege of tracing the importance of the blood throughout the Old Testament. Let's consider the spiritual implications of these true accounts of God's people who lived before us.

ABRAHAM

Genesis 22 is the record of Abraham's test of faith. God ordered him to take his only son and offer him as a sacrifice in a place he would be directed to. Without question Abraham followed instructions to sacrifice his son, Isaac in the land of Moriah. Three things Abraham said are significant.

1. The first was the instructions he gave to the servants traveling with them.

"Stay here with the donkey. The lad and I will go yonder and worship, and we will come back to you."

This is what we call faith-talk. Abraham didn't understand but He trusted God.

2. The second statement was made to his son when Isaac questioned his father.

"Look, the fire and the wood, but where is the lamb for a burnt offering?"

Abraham replied,

"My son, God will provide for Himself the lamb for a burnt offering."

There's no use trying to understand this with our human reasoning. You cannot. We do know, of course, God stopped Abraham just as he was prepared to kill Isaac. At that moment he saw a ram caught by its horns and offered it instead of his son. When we first heard this true story we all breathed a big sigh of relief. However, God's Son did not get rescued at Calvary. There was no sigh of relief as Jesus was nailed to the cross and lifted up to die as a substitute for you and me. The price of blood had to be paid. Jesus, the perfect Son of God did this for us. He was the only one who could qualify – the innocent for the guilty.

This prophetic picture gives us an idea of the Father's heart when His only Son Jesus was nailed to a cross. It also shows us the meaning of John 3:16.

"For God so loved the world that He gave His only begotten son that whoever believes in Him will not perish but have eternal life."

3. The third thing Abraham said was to call the name of the place,

"The LORD-Will-Provide, as it is said to this day, In the Mount of the LORD it shall be provided." Genesis 22:14.

This mountain in Jerusalem later became the exact place God sacrificed His own Son, Jesus on a cross between two thieves.

MOSES

In Exodus 12, we read about the institution of the Passover on the night before Moses led the Israelites out of Egyptian bondage. The LORD instructed Moses to tell the people to take a male lamb without blemish and kill it, putting some blood on the doorposts of their house before it was roasted and eaten.

"Now the blood shall be a sign for you on the houses where you are and when I see the blood I will pass over you and the plague shall not be on you to destroy you when I strike the land of Egypt."
Exodus 12:13

Throughout the years thousands upon thousands of animals were sacrificed to the Lord, each one a little picture of the One who would come as the ultimate sacrifice. When King Solomon dedicated the temple he built for God he offered a sacrifice of 22,000 bulls and 120,000 sheep. (1 Kings 8:63) Hebrews 9:22 teaches us that without the shedding of blood there can be no forgiveness. Question: If you were God, what would you do to show your people the importance of the blood? Do you think the blood of the sacrifice lamb says it clearly?

The sacrifice system was still in place at the time Jesus was nailed to the cross. He died the same day Jewish priests were killing sacrificial lambs in Jerusalem. Jesus Christ was, as John the Baptist declared,

"Behold, the Lamb of God who takes away the sin of the world." John 1:29

Isaiah prophesied about this hundreds of years before in Isaiah 53:6.

"All we like sheep have gone astray. We have turned, everyone, to his own way, and the LORD (God) has laid on Him (Jesus) the iniquity of us all."

As a follower of Jesus, we need to be reminded of the power of the blood that not only provides for salvation initially, but keeps on saving us every day. There are other promises concerning the blood that are important for us to understand.

"For if when we were enemies we were reconciled to God through the death of His Son, much more, having been

reconciled, we shall be saved by His life." Romans 5:10

The word reconciled means exchange. This is the great exchange – my sins for His righteousness; your sins for His righteousness.

"For He (God) made Him (Jesus) who knew no sin to be sin for us that we might become the righteousness of God in Him." 2 Corinthians 5:21

Reconciliation is the process by which God and man are brought together. This is much more than friendship. Through the blood of Jesus, who was 100% perfect without sin, we are made joint-heirs with Christ, sons and daughters of the Most High. Not only saved from the penalty of sin for eternity, but saved from the power of sin today. Sin can no longer rule over you. The price for this "so great salvation" is the shed blood of Jesus. The blood of Christ is forever the only means of right relationship with the Holy God. That's the power of the blood that keeps on continually cleansing you day after day. (1 John 1:7) This is so completely opposite from our human way of thinking it can be hard to comprehend. Why would God give His only Son for such as you or such as I? Salvation costs us nothing. It is a gift… this eternal life we are offered. The price is more costly than our minds can possibly understand – the life-blood of our Savior, Jesus Christ.

Let's look at a Scripture that explains the gospel of victory – the ultimate result of a believer who fights the good fight of obedient faith and wins.

"And they (believers) overcame him (the enemy) by the blood of the Lamb and by the word of their testimony…"
Revelation 12:11

As I have said before, to be an overcomer suggests combat against the enemy through Jesus Christ, the victorious Warrior. "The battle is the Lord's", as David said to Goliath just before he threw the rock that killed the giant.

One of the most outlandish realities in a believer's life and struggles is failure to respond to the very presence of God in our life. Every true believer has the Holy Spirit of God living on the inside, along with grace to overcome any and all obstacles. This must be what the writer of Hebrews meant to "neglect so great salvation." (2:3) He issues a warning to give careful attention to the things we have been taught or we could "drift away", picturing a ship drifting past safe anchorage into danger.

Have you found it easy to drift? To simply go with the flow without making waves; follow the majority; go with the crowd; keep your mouth shut; stay away from controversial topics. To stand against evil requires great courage in today's culture war.

When Jesus instituted the Lord's Supper during the last Jewish Passover celebration with his disciples He gave thanks, broke the bread and said,

"Take, eat, this is My body broken for you."

After supper He took the cup, saying,

"This cup is the new covenant in My blood."

After each element He gave one important command that is to be a guiding light for believers today:

"Do this in remembrance of Me."

God is pleased when a believer acknowledges the triumphant victory of the cross. Jesus' body was bruised, broken, and bleeding. His own life-blood was poured out unto death. Jesus paid it all and He did it for you. He did it for me.

Today we overcome because God has declared believers righteous and victorious through the blood of His Son, Jesus. All charges against us were paid in full. The blood has set us free. This is what Jesus meant when He cried from the cross, "It is finished!" The work He was sent to do was completed once and for all and the results live on continually and victoriously! There's victory in the blood!

"Thanks be to God who gives us the victory through our Lord Jesus Christ."

1 Corinthians 15:57

CHAPTER 7

VICTORY THROUGH STRENGTH

"...let the weak say I am strong..."
Joel 3:10

Strength is a word you probably have not looked up in Webster's Dictionary. We know strength means to be strong; to have power; to be tough; to endure, but most will admit there are times when we feel weak, helpless, or lacking in some way. However, there is a secret involved for those who follow Jesus Christ. It will require effort or ability to choose God's way of obtaining strength.

David wrote Psalm 18, to express his thanks to God for giving him strength.

"I will love You, O LORD, my strength."

He tells of God being his rock, his fortress, his

deliverer, his shield, and how God answered his prayer when he was helpless, without strength. In verse 32, he writes,

"It is God who arms me with strength and makes my way perfect."

Here's the key, found in Nehemiah 8:10b.

"…The joy of the Lord is your strength."

To get the full implication of this word from God the word "strong" in the dictionary can enlarge our understanding of its importance to our lives. Strong is a big word involving our total being – body, soul, and spirit, along with the mind, emotions, and the will. God wants His people to be in a healthy and sound condition; to be morally powerful with strength of character; to think clearly; to walk in firm authority; to endure and resist temptation; and to make a difference. The joy of the Lord is our source for strength.

Definition of Joy

The question we need to ask is, what is the joy of the Lord? I'm sure you know we're not thinking about happiness, which depends on what happens to you, or your current circumstances. Joy is a deep sense of well being in spite of circumstances. The only source for joy is God. It is being confident in knowing He is in control, He's got your back! Although the joy of the Lord is certainly available to every believer, it is something you must choose. Choose joy! We must cultivate and promote the joy of the Lord as a powerful source of spiritual strength. This joy is promised. The key is relationship, relationship, relationship.

King David had many ups and downs during his life but one of the most revealing scriptures about how he handled trouble, disappointment, and heartache is found in 1 Samuel 30:6b.

"...But David strengthened himself in the LORD his God."

Today we might say, David threw himself into his work, or David went on an extended vacation. These are human fixes at best. Are you listening?

In the face of terrible circumstances David knew where to go. He found strength in the Lord.

One of the great examples of pure joy is found in Acts 16, where Paul and Silas were thrown into prison for delivering a demon-possessed girl from the kingdom of darkness into God's Kingdom of Light. Although they suffered from the beating with Roman whips, this is what is recorded in Acts 16:25.

"At midnight Paul and Silas were praying and singing hymns to God..."

In spite of the terrible circumstances these men of God maintained their joy. Of course, you know the end results were that God sent an earthquake to open prison doors and set them free. The icing on the cake is the salvation of the keeper of the prison and his family after he cried out to Paul, "What must I do to be saved?" Come on class, you know the answer to this one. This was the greatest victory possible.

Acts 16:31, "Believe on the Lord Jesus Christ, and you will be saved."

"Now when he (the jailer) had brought them into his house, he set food before them: and he rejoiced, having believed in God with all his household." Acts 16:34

I suggest to you today, you will need the joy only Jesus can give in days to come.

Another example of the joy of the Lord is found in Acts 13:52. Paul and Barnabus were having success in preaching in the city of Antioch when a violent mob of Jews opposed them and drove them out of the city.

"And the disciples were filled with joy and with the Holy Spirit."

The Secret of Joy

- Abide in Him. Jesus points the way to joy in John 15:10, 11.

"If you keep My commandments you will abide in My love, just as I have kept My Father's commandments and

abide in His love. These things I have spoken to you that my joy may remain in you and that your joy may be full."

David wrote Psalm 16:11.

"You will show me the path of life: in Your presence is fullness of joy: at Your right hand there are pleasures forever."

- Be filled with the Holy Spirit.
  The joy of the Lord is rooted in relationship with the Holy Spirit. Joy is a fruit and a sign to the world. (Galatians 5)

  We are instructed in Ephesians 5:18, to be continually being filled with the Spirit. Since this is the Person of God the Holy Spirit, you don't get more of Him, rather He gets more of you. Let Him fill every fiber of your being and you will discover joy – real joy – wonderful joy.

How does one maintain joy?

1. "Count your blessings, see what God has done", to quote from an old hymn. Keep these before you with a heart of thanksgiving. Write them – make a list of specific things God has already done.

2. Be around joyful people. Joy is contagious. Do you know someone you love to be with because they are full of joy? Try to be that joyful friend for someone.

3. Simply believe!

"(Jesus) whom having not seen you love though you do not see Him, yet believing, you rejoice with joy inexpressible and full of glory." 1 Peter 1:8,9

Doubt and unbelief are constantly at war with obedient faith in Jesus Christ. Understanding and obeying God's Word brings great joy.

Joy Robbers

Perhaps it's time to pull out the trusty little Joy-O-Meter and test your level of joy. Joy should be a gage for how you're doing over-all. It's one of the first indicators of being filled with the Spirit.

The opposite of joy is sadness, sorrow, being miserable. Without joy you may become desperate, despondent, depressed, weighed down, yes, even hopeless. This must be high on the job description of the devil. He is the master joy robber. If he can get you to shrink into weakness he can fulfill his plan to steal, kill, and destroy your purpose in life.

The Joy-Giver lives in you and He's not going anywhere. Acknowledge His presence. Become God-inside minded. Stay on the path of joy.

Ask yourself two questions:

1. When do I feel most joyful? Remember, don't confuse joy and happiness.
2. When do I feel least joyful? The answers may help you to discover things that rob you of joy.

Example of King David

David knew the joy of the Lord. He freely worshiped with music and dance. What happened to cause David to cry out to God in Psalm 51:12a?

"Return me to the joy of Your salvation."

We know the story. David sinned against God by having an adulterous affair with Bathsheba, trying to cover it up by having her husband killed in battle, resulting in God sending a prophet to confront him with this sin against God. Only then (a year or so later) did David confess his sin and turn back to God for forgiveness. In Psalm 21:1, David wrote,

"The king shall joy in thy strength, O LORD: and in thy salvation how greatly shall he rejoice!"

David's joy was restored when he prayed, and praised God, and worshiped. He wrote Psalm 27:1, 6.

"The Lord is the strength of my life...I will offer sacrifices of joy in His tabernacle. I will sing, yes, I will sing praises to the Lord."

Example of The Apostle Peter

Peter surely knew the joy of the Lord. What caused him to lose his joy? Again, sin. He denied knowing the Lord with cursing and swearing oaths. (Matthew 26:69-75) We can only imagine the great joy that was restored to Peter after the resurrection.

Example of believers today

There's one message believers who are awake and watchful during this season are hearing repeatedly: Strengthen your relationship with Jesus Christ. Draw near to Him. Live in His presence moment by moment. You cannot make it on your own. Everything we need is in Jesus. Last days events are upon us. We must not drift away from our God and Savior now. Yes, we are being tested and tried and we will come through like gold, so don't give up, back up, or fall down. You know the end of the story.

If you and I are to experience victory through strength what are we to take from this chapter? The secret to your strength is the joy of the Lord! Look to Jesus, the Author and Finisher of our faith who said, "My joy I give to you."

To summarize let's consider Philippians 4:13.

"I can do all things through Christ who strengthens me."

"Thanks be to God who gives us the victory through our Lord Jesus Christ."

1 Corinthians 15:57

CHAPTER 8

VICTORY OVER THE TONGUE

I have to admit this continues to be a struggle for me, perhaps because of misinformation or a wrong concept of what it means to be "in Christ". Just as I was taught a believer has no authority, it stands to reason the words I speak carry no weight either. This was the unspoken attitude I picked up as a child. I have had to unlearn some things I got wrong in earlier years.

It's really a matter of getting into the Word of God and believing what He says. To have victory over the words you speak begins with seeing the need to change. No change ever takes place until you want to change. Only then will you turn it over to God and allow the Holy Spirit to work in your heart the truth that sets you free.

Psalms 19:14 "Let the words of my mouth and the meditation of my heart

be acceptable in Your sight O LORD,
my strength and my Redeemer."

This Psalm reveals the heart of a man with a sincere desire to please God. We know God answered this prayer when David was called, "A man after God's own heart."

A new believer learns not to use the Lord's name as a curse word. Then you realize talking bad about another believer is wrong. Next, gossip becomes a problem, or maybe dirty jokes and filthy words. The Holy Spirit is at work teaching us the principals of godly living. It seems really strange to me when a believer continues to talk trash – or tells crude jokes. I realize this comes from my upbringing, thanks to my mother. These are areas the Holy Spirit cleans up fairly quickly. But just how far does this go – the battle over the tongue?

Proverbs 18:21 may give us a clue.

"Death and life are in the power of the tongue and those who love it will eat its fruit."

What does it mean to speak life or to speak death? To speak life is to speak what God has to say on any issue. It doesn't matter what I think or what you think. What does God say?

"Without faith it is impossible to please God." Hebrews 11:6

To speak death is to speak negative thoughts, to declare defeat, or to complain constantly. How does this sound? "I can't do anything right"; "You don't have a lick of sense"; "I can't win for losing"; "They're killing me"; I'm falling apart one piece at a time"; "Those preachers are just out to get your money". Some of us grew up with this kind of loose talk as everyday conversation. No one took the words seriously. They were just idle words. Little did we know! Beware of casual conversation when it turns to loose talk.

To try to off-set negative words one large segment of the church began saying a most irritating cliché, "I'm blessed!" No matter what the conversation was about someone would say, "Oh, I'm blessed." This, of course is true if spoken from the heart. In some cases, it is just meaningless words. No one would dare ask, "How are you – really?" Most of the time you didn't want to know anyway.

Whatever the motive for several years every time someone said, "I'm blessed", it left me feeling embarrassed or somehow inferior. I wanted to say, "Excuse me!" O.K., I've revealed an area that you probably recognize as Speech 101, in the School of the Kingdom. Please accept my apology. What in the world was I thinking? Do you realize how many verses there are that teach us about how blessed a believer really is? Father has just pulled me up by the bootstraps and I'm ready for a quick and permanent correction. "I'm blessed!" Say it. "I'm blessed!" Aren't you thankful that our Heavenly Father continues teaching us – loving us – extending His mercy to us every day? He continues to say, "Words matter!"

Just to remind us of how big the word blessed really is let's look at several of the powerful promises the Word of God gives.

James 1:12 "Blessed is the man who endures temptation; for when he has been approved he will receive the crown of life, which the Lord has promised to those who love Him."

This is not all there is. We must not allow circumstances of life to draw us away from God. Instead, don't be tempted to run away from God, but when a trial comes run quickly into the safety of God's arms. You'll be blessed.

James 1:25 "But he who looks into the perfect law of liberty (the Word of God) and continues in it, and is not a forgetful hearer, but a doer of the work, this one will be blessed in what he does."

This scripture puts emphasis on obedient faith. In The Passion Translation, Proverbs 18:21 reads, "Your words are so powerful that they will kill or give life and the talkative person will reap the consequences."

When the Holy Spirit begins to work on this area it's time to put in some altar-time. Repent and change. We've got to get this right. Words matter! We have the written record of what Jesus says about the importance of what we say. It's not just a matter of sounding words; rather it is a heart issue.

> "...For out of the abundance of the heart the mouth speaks...I say to you that for every idle word men speak, they will give account of it in the day of judgment. For by your words you will be justified, and by your words you will be condemned." Matthew 12:34b, 36, 37.

If you want to know the character of a man or woman listen to the words he speaks. What's on the inside comes out in the way you talk. In this chapter Jesus said good things come from the heart of a good man.

> "So above all, guard the affections of your heart (with determined effort) for they affect all that you are. Pay close attention to the welfare of your innermost

being for from there flows the wellspring of life." Proverbs 4:23 TPT

Why are there so many warnings about the heart? God's love won't allow one of His children to fail. He knows your talk can cancel out your walk. Words can cancel the precious promises God has given. It grieves the Holy Spirit of God when we carelessly speak idle (worthless) words. God created vocal cords for victory. You can have victory over the tongue!

James, the brother of Jesus speaks most emphatically concerning the dangers involved by careless speech. James himself was an unbeliever until the resurrection of Jesus, but he must have heard Jesus teach. I like to think his mother, Mary, had something to do with his spiritual growth as well. James would have been with the 120 in the Upper Room on the Day of Pentecost and later became the leader of the church in Jerusalem. Beginning in James 3, he writes of the untamable tongue.

"But no man can tame the tongue. It is an unruly evil, full of deadly poison." (3:8)

He explains how the power of the tongue can influence for good or bad even though it is a small member of the body. He compares the tongue to a small fire that can burn a forest; a bit put in a horse's mouth to control it; a small rudder that can turn a large ship; and a spring that produces both good and impure water.

"For we all stumble in many things. If anyone does not stumble in word, he is a perfect (mature) man, able also to bridle the whole body. (3:2)

"Thanks be to God who gives us the victory through our Lord Jesus Christ."

1 Corinthians 15:57

CHAPTER 9
VICTORY IN YOUR WALK

The word "walk" in the Bible dictionary simply means to live a life. I'll never forget the first time this word came to my attention. I was sitting under the dryer at my weekly beauty shop visit and my eyes were drawn to a little Christian magazine on the table with all the other major publications. The cover picture was a simple path with tiny footprints walking up a hill. The caption in bold letters read, Walk Worthy.

I quickly turned the page to the editorial on the inside cover. The words were electrifying.

"I therefore, the prisoner of the Lord, beseech you to walk worthy of the calling with which you were called."
Ephesians 4:1

I began to cry – no, sob is a more appropriate description. Hiding behind the magazine I tried to compose myself, but it wasn't going to happen. What was going on? I didn't even understand what walk worthy meant, but at that moment those words were speaking volumes. Ephesians 4:1, became my life-verse. Through the years it has continued to guide me, often meaning different things according to the season. Each time I look into its meaning I learn more. My pastor often says, "The word does not change, but we do."

"Worthy" means suitable, appropriate, or deserving. Believers want to live up to the Name of Jesus. God has given us a standard to follow as we seek to live worthy of His Name. That standard is the Word of God. That standard is Jesus, the Word made flesh. (John 1:14)

What about this calling? Perhaps you may be thinking as I did, it is referring to your vocation. In Ephesians 4:1, God is reminding us of so great salvation bought and paid for by the precious life-blood of Jesus, and given as a free gift to anyone who comes to Him by faith.

The question we all face at one time or another is, how can I possibly be worthy of such a gift? That's a question the Holy Spirit of God loves to answer. You can't! I can't! It's not about you and I being worthy. Jesus is the Worthy One.

When one comes to God for forgiveness of sin we were immediately placed "in Christ". From that moment on it's all about Him – who He is and what He will do for us. This could possibly be the hardest truth we are asked to believe. The sooner you become God-inside minded, the more victory you will experience day by day. We are in Him and Christ is in each believer. This is accomplished by the power of the abiding presence of God, the Holy Spirit who comes to live inside. One of the great and mighty promises we have been given is Hebrews 13:5.

"I will never leave you nor forsake you."

Do you remember the story of a young man who decided to take his inheritance and leave the boring safety of his father's house so he could go far away and live it up? This is recorded in Luke 15. He was a privileged younger son that felt he didn't need anyone telling him how to live his life. After he had blown all his money bad times hit the land and he had nothing left. He ended up feeding pigs and sharing their slop. There in the pig pen he came to himself and remembered his Father's love and the good life he had left behind.

He began rehearsing what he would say if he got back home.

"Father, I have sinned against heaven and before you, and I'm no longer worthy to be called your son..." Luke 15:18, 19

No longer worthy! Was he ever worthy? Oh yes, he was safe and secure in His Father's love, but he left it all for the fleeting pleasures of this world. Could he dare to hope he could go back to his Father and be received as a lowly servant?

Have you ever felt unworthy – undeserving of being a child of God? The Father was watching for his son to return – waiting with open arms – wanting his son to come to his senses. You and I will never be worthy. Because of God's unfailing love, if you have received Jesus as Savior, the Worthy One lives in you. The most important lesson to take from this true story is your invitation to do the impossible – again. Remember Jesus Himself said, "Without Me you can do nothing." (John 15:5) By the power of the Holy Spirit you can live a life that pleases God. This is the Father's plan to equip you to walk worthy of so great salvation!

There is only one way to fail in your spiritual walk and that is to refuse God's invitation to walk worthy. Consider another word from God in Colossians 1:9 – 14. I see five things the Holy Spirit says it takes to walk worthy.

"For this reason we...do not cease to pray for you and to ask that you may be filled with the knowledge of His will in all wisdom and spiritual understanding that you may walk worthy of the Lord fully pleasing Him. being fruitful in every good work and increasing in the knowledge of God. strengthened with all might according to His glorious power for all patience and longsuffering with joy. giving thanks to the Father who has qualified us to be partakers of the inheritance of the saints of light. He has delivered us from the power of darkness

and conveyed (transferred) us into the Kingdom of the Son of His love, in whom we have redemption through His blood, the forgiveness of sins."

1. Filled with the knowledge of His will. How can one know God's will? I searched for several years to know God's will for my life, going here and there and seeking answers from church leaders. The answer I found is, "to ask". God's will is not a secret being kept from you. He wants to reveal His will for your life, and it will be specific for you alone. Your part is to ask. When you sincerely desire to please God, to obey what He says in His Word, He will reveal exactly what He wants you to do. "Ask, and it will be given to you; seek and you will find; knock and it will be opened to you." Matthew 7:7

2. Having wisdom and spiritual understanding. As a matter of fact, you have already been given all things that have to do with life and godliness according to 2 Peter 1:3.

"His divine power has given to us all things that pertain to life and godliness, through the knowledge of Him that has called us to glory and virtue." Your part is to align yourself accordingly. You must receive by faith everything God has freely given. Believe God's Word.

3. A life that pleases God.
   This means a productive life continually growing in knowing our Lord. We have been given this word and let me say this much. It's not a suggestion.

*"Grow in the grace and knowledge of our Lord and Savior Jesus Christ."
2 Peter 3:18*

4. Receive God's abundant grace.
   To walk worthy will also include God's strength along with the desire and the power to do His will.

5. Always give thanks.

"And let the peace of God rule in your heart... and be thankful." Colossians 3:15

The Spirit wants us to never forget to keep the main thing the main thing. Be thankful! Our Heavenly Father alone is responsible for including you in His divine plan of salvation. He delivered you from the power of darkness and transferred you into the Kingdom of His Son. It is through the precious blood of Jesus you have a continual cleansing and day by day forgiveness of sin.

My dear friend, if you are still reading this I sense you want to be successful in your spiritual life. We know each of us will one day stand before our Father, and our precious Lord Jesus to answer for the decisions being made today. Let me encourage you with this final scripture from 1 Thessalonians 5:24. God's got this! Walk in victory today.

"Faithful is He who called you who also will perform it."

"*Thanks be to God who gives us the victory through our Lord Jesus Christ.*"

1 Corinthians 15:57

CHAPTER 10

VICTORY OVER THE REAL YOU

I'm fairly sure you've heard the little story of a white dog and a black dog that fought constantly. Someone asked the owner how he knew which dog would win. His answer, "It's always the one I feed the most."

Corny? Perhaps, but very applicable to the Christian life. You see, the white dog and the black dog are both you.

When anyone comes to faith in Jesus Christ you begin at the cross where you experience a new birth. The white dog is born, you might say. This faith in Jesus Christ is a complete reliance on Him, trusting Him rather than oneself for salvation thus making salvation an entirely free gift of God rather than through any good works of your own. (Ephesians 2:8, 9) The little white dog will need good nourishment and care to grow strong and healthy. You must make wise choices and be deliberate in your spiritual development.

Nevertheless, you have been born again and have become a new creation in Christ and placed into a covenant circle of His love, His provision, and His protection. (Titus 2:14)

> *"For He (God) made Him (Jesus) who knew no sin to be sin for us, that we (believers) might become the righteousness of God in Him (Jesus). 2 Corinthians 5:21*

Jesus, the sinless One took all our sins in Himself on the cross, enduring the penalty that we deserve – separation from a holy God. He became the substitute for all mankind.

> *"Christ died for our sins according to the Scriptures, and that He was buried, and that He rose again the third day..." 1 Corinthians 15:3, 4*

When by faith you believe in Jesus Christ, according to God's Word many things happen. It will be very advantageous for us to examine these truths more fully in order to embrace the real you – now a new creation in Christ.

You are saved. To redeem from sin – Jesus paid the price with His life-blood. Ephesians 2:8 "For by grace (underserved love of God) you have been saved through faith…"

You are born-again. To put your trust in Jesus and changed by the power of the Holy Spirit working through the Word of God.
1 Peter 1:23 "For you have been born again… through the living and enduring word of God.

You are washed. To be cleansed from all sin: past, present, future.
1 Corinthians 6:11 "…But you were washed…in the Name of the Lord Jesus and by the Spirit of our God."

You are forgiven. From all offenses against God. Colossians 2:13 "And you…He has made alive together with Him, having forgiven you all trespasses."

You are justified. Declared free from blame; accepted by God.

Romans 3:24 "Being justified freely by His grace through the redemption that is in Christ Jesus."

You are a new creation. Created in Christ Jesus. 2 Corinthians 5:17 "If anyone is in Christ, he is a new creation; old things have passed away; behold, all things have become new."

You are like a newborn baby. You will immediately begin to grow up.
1 Peter 2:2 "As newborn babes, desire the pure milk of the word that you may grow thereby."

You have eternal life. Beginning now and forever.
1 John 5:13 "These things I have written to you who believe in the name of the Son of God, that you may know that you have eternal life and that you may continue to believe…"

You are a work of art. Designed by God, the Master Designer.
Ephesians 2:10 "For we are His workmanship, created in Christ Jesus…"

You are called. To be part of the eternal Kingdom of God.

Ephesians 4:1 "I…beseech you to walk worthy of the calling with which you were called."

God lives in you.
1 John 4:12 "…God abides in us, and His love has been perfected in us."

You are a child of God.
Galatians 3:26 "For you are all sons of God through faith in Christ Jesus."

Christ Jesus is in you.
Ephesians 3:17 "That Christ may dwell in your hearts through faith…"

You are complete in Christ Jesus.
Colossians 2:9, 10 "For in Him dwells all the fullness of the Godhead bodily; and you are complete in Him…"

You have access to Jesus.
Ephesians 3:12 "We have boldness and access with confidence through faith in Him."

You are continually cleansed from sin day after day.

1 John 1:7 "...the blood of Jesus Christ His Son cleanses us from all sin."

Jesus is praying for you bringing requests to the Father.
Romans 8:34 "...it is Christ who died, is also risen, who is even at the right hand of God, who also makes intercession for us."

Your citizenship is in heaven.
Philippians 3:20 "For our citizenship is in heaven from which we also eagerly wait for the Savior, the Lord Jesus Christ."

God hears you pray.
1 Peter 3:12 "For the eyes of the Lord are on the righteous, and His ears are open to their prayers..."

You have angels with you every day.
Psalm 91:11 "For He shall give His angels charge over you to keep you in all your ways."

You are dead to sin. No longer being ruled/controlled by sin.

Romans 6:11 "...reckon (count as factual) yourselves to be dead to sin but alive to God in Christ Jesus our Lord."

The Holy Spirit lives in you. He is God.
1 Corinthians 6:19 "Do you not know that your body is the temple of the Holy Spirit who is in you, whom you have from God..."

God will never leave you. You can enjoy His constant presence.
Hebrews 13:5 "...He Himself has said, I will never leave you nor forsake you."

The real you is being renewed daily. Exchanging weakness for His strength.
2 Corinthians 4:16 "The inward man is being renewed day by day."

You are sanctified. Set apart as God's own child.
1 Corinthians 6:11 "You were washed...you were sanctified...you were justified in the Name of the Lord Jesus and by the Spirit of our God."

Since you and I were created with a mind, emotions, and a will these continue to operate in our lives after the new birth. Now you have the great advantage of God-inside always there to help you. You continue to have a choice in how you live and whether to please God or to please yourself.

The mind has a mind of its own, often demanding its way rather than God's way. Your mind must be renewed to the Word of God so you will have a desire and the power to do God's will. You must choose to walk in the Spirit and live a life under the control and power of the Holy Spirit, who lives in you. This means war! Yes, we are called to war against the flesh. I'm sure you have discovered this to be your greatest enemy.

As an important reminder, let's look once again at 2 Peter 1:3.

"As His divine power has given to us all things that pertain to life and godliness...through the knowledge of Him who called us by glory and virtue."

Shall we go back to basics! <u>The key to every victory is found in knowing Jesus</u>. Paul's heart cry was that he could know Him and the power of His resurrection. (Philippians 3:10) Did Paul know

Christ? Yes, of course he did. Paul experienced the new birth through a supernatural encounter on the road to Damascus where he planned to arrest and imprison followers of Christ. He learned the only thing that really mattered was to know Jesus more intimately. He came to love Jesus for who He is, loving His presence and enjoying God's favor on his life. Paul continued to be a seeker of more his entire life.

There's a little known fact that's important for you to understand why we as believers in Jesus Christ continue to mess up. Are you ready for a secret? Pay close attention – the black dog is not dead! You may not be aware you have been feeding him. Everything in the world system of this century feeds him: T.V., movies, magazines, the arts, public schools, the media, and all your numerous devices. The greatest enemy of all is on the inside – the mind. With a constant diet of garbage, guess what's going to come out. As the old saying goes: Garbage in! Garbage out!

It's important to remember the flesh is weak. The black dog shows he is stronger than we first imagined. The flesh wants to sin. The flesh wants to control. God hates the flesh and the flesh hates

God. The only hope is found in the flesh being controlled by the Holy Spirit.

Walk in the Spirit and you will not obey the flesh. Be continually filled with the Holy Spirit. He will guide you into all truth – drawing you closer and closer to our Lord Jesus. These are things God has promised all who believe.

Around 1980, Tim LaHaye, Pastor of Scott Memorial Baptist Church in San Diego (before David Jeremiah), wrote a best seller, Battle for the Mind. At the time it sent shock waves throughout the church. Then, twenty years later he wrote a follow-up, The Siege, revealing even more shocking statistics of the condition of the church. (By the way, the church is you and me and all believers throughout the world.) Today, re-reading that book is like watching tonight's news. The worst is already happening all around us. This would look pretty hopeless if not for the truth we know in Matthew 16:18. Jesus said,

"I will build My church and the gates of hell will not prevail against it!"

Today the Holy Spirit of God is giving

encouragement to the body of Christ to stay in there – do not give up. We have the victory, right?

Believe it or not, Christian standards are in complete opposition to the world system. A recent report by George Barna revealed that only 4% of those claiming to be Christian parents hold to a Biblical worldview. This means 96% do not believe God's Word. I wanted to know exactly what is considered a Biblical worldview. This is what I found.

1. **God is the Creator.**
   Genesis 1:1 "In the beginning God created the heavens and the earth."

2. **The Bible, the Word of God is the absolute authority, without error.**
   2 Timothy 3:16, 17 "All Scripture is given by inspiration of God, and is profitable

   for doctrine, for reproof, for correction, for instruction in righteousness that the man of God may be complete, thoroughly equipped…"

3. **Moral truth exists.**
These are indisputable values of the born-again lifestyle: righteousness (correct standing before God); faith (trusting God completely); and love (of God and His Church). 2 Timothy 2:22 "Flee also youthful lusts; but pursue righteousness, faith, love, peace with those who call on the Lord out of a pure heart."

4. **Jesus, God's only sinless Son died on the cross, was buried, and rose again.**
1 Corinthians 15:3, 4 "…Christ died for our sins according to the Scriptures, He was buried, and He rose again the 3rd day."

5. **Satan is the enemy of God and man.**
1 Peter 5:8 "Be sober, be vigilant; because your adversary the devil walks about like a roaring lion seeking whom he may devour."

6. **Salvation is by faith alone.**
Ephesians 2:8, 9 "For by grace you have been saved through faith, and that not of yourselves; it is the gift of God, not of works, lest anyone should boast."

The age-old question remains: Is it important what you believe? If you are to have victory over the mind you must believe the truth. God's Word is the only truth available. Knowing the truth protects you from lies and deception.

John 8:32 teaches that we can know the truth by personal, intimate experience. It is the Truth you know that sets you free. Are you walking in the Truth?

This takes us back to why God gave us a mind to think, emotions to feel, and a will to decide. This is how you learn. For example, let's look at this basic truth concerning God's love.

The Mind

First, you must hear the truth. God loves you. Maybe you sang "Jesus loves me, this I know, for the Bible tells me so." You may have heard John 3:16. God so loved _me_ that He gave His only Son (Jesus) that if _I_ believe in Him __I__ would have everlasting life. This truth has evidence. You learned that Jesus died for your sins, in your place. Who could love you that much? That's a lot to think about.

The Emotions

When you hear the truth your emotions will get involved. Does God really love me? Now you must decide?

Ephesians 1:13 "In Him you also trusted, after you heard the word of truth, the gospel of your salvation..."

2 Thessalonians 2:10 tells us many will be deceived and will not receive the love of the truth that they might be saved. These choose to love sin instead of God's Son. As you can see, learning is always in stages. First, you hear and your mind thinks about what you've heard. Then you receive what you've heard. Yes, God loves me. I believe Jesus is my Savior and gave His life-blood for me. This is real love.

The Will

The final step involves the will. Each of us has a free will to decide for ourselves to receive the truth of God's love. This is where the truth becomes reality and shows up in every area of your life. When you know God loves you and you believe Christ died for you, was buried, and came to life again—all for you, your natural response will be to love God back. Jesus said, "If you love Me you will obey the truth." Your will says, "I will follow Jesus Christ. I will obey." Now you begin to walk in obedient faith. And the fight goes on!

When you have trouble walking in truth, obeying what God says, remember the cross. Remember His love. Repent and turn back to God. He is always ready to forgive one of His children.

"If we confess our sins He is faithful and just to forgive us our sins and to cleanse us from all unrighteousness."
1 John 1:9

"Thanks be to God who gives us the victory through our Lord Jesus Christ."

1 Corinthians 15:57

CHAPTER 11
VICTORY IN
HARD TIMES

If you were asked to describe hard times what would you say? Several years ago I wrote an entire book called Living in your Fortified Place, to offer some small piece of advice to a world gone crazy. This is on the back cover: People today are feeling the effects of the many dangers facing our world. Fear, anxiety, anger and hopelessness fill the hearts of many who are seeking answers. It is important to be reminded that Almighty God has not abandoned His people. He has a perfect plan in place and everything will be accomplished according to His perfect will.

Since that time an entirely new dictionary has been written to include words never before coined to describe hard times in a post-Christian society. Where does it go from here?

Hard times come in many forms. There are as many categories of trouble or suffering as there are people. In the book of James you will find many of the various circumstances we find ourselves experiencing today. He begins in 1:2.

"Count it all joy when you fall into various trials."

This scripture may turn you off if your fail to get the meaning behind the words. First notice the word "when" is used instead of "if"—when you fall into various trials. In other words, everyone gets some. No one is left out. It's just a matter of time so be prepared.

Well, that little bit of information didn't help much did it? When you get right down to facts you will have to admit it's true. I don't know one single person who is either now or has recently faced difficult times. The next thing James says is that this is a test of your faith. It seems a major issue here has to do with attitude. We are instructed to choose how we're going to deal with circumstances facing us, "count it all joy." For this to become our reality we have to see the bigger picture.

First of all it helps to know this trial is temporary. Acknowledging the presence of Jesus is vital. He is always our "ever-present help" for any and every need. (Psalm 46:1)

Recently I was studying James 1, seeking a deeper understanding and a personal application when I discovered something very interesting in Hebrews 12:1.

"Let us run with perseverance (endurance, patience) the race marked out for us (or set up before us)."

To make sure I got the full meaning I had to look up the word perseverance. It's more than to keep going. It means the ability to overcome various tests and trials that are meant to expose the weak, undisciplined areas in our lives. Another meaning is to continue to bear up under difficult circumstances. In other words, never give up! Then it came to me – the purpose for trials and tribulations (sorrow, hardship, grief, suffering) is to make us more like Jesus. I am not saying God brings difficulty into our lives or that He is responsible for them, rather that He never leaves us and He can use our problems as tools to accomplish His purpose. That's how Paul could say all things work together for good to those who love God. (Romans 8:28)

Our Heavenly Father has a plan all marked out before us. Each of us is uniquely His and is on a specific journey through life. Hard times will come but they cannot change God's perfect plan and our destiny.

We can look to the Apostle Paul as an excellent example. As an unbeliever He persecuted the followers of Jesus. When He was saved Jesus said this about Paul.

"I will show him how many things he must suffer for My name's sake." Acts 9:16.

Hard times began for Paul (Saul of Tarsus) almost immediately as the Jews looked for a way to kill him. In 1 Corinthians 11:23-28, Paul openly shared the hardships as well as victories of following Jesus. Much of what he suffered happened after he wrote this book but he tells of hard work; arrests; being beaten and stoned; shipwrecked and lost at sea; many of his dangerous trips through wilderness, across oceans, and in enemy territory; hunger and thirst and being cold without proper clothing, etc. He certainly qualifies to give advice on the subject of victory in hard times.

Trials, when handled properly, are meant to produce spiritual growth. The goal is to become mature followers of Jesus Christ – with "nothing missing and nothing lacking". TPT

The testing of our faith stirs up power within us to make us strong enough to endure all things. (James 1:3) This is a great scripture from The Passion Translation, in James 1:12.

"If your faith remains strong, even while surrounded by life's difficulties, you will continue to experience the untold blessings of God. True happiness comes as you pass the test with faith, and receive the victorious crown of life promised to every lover of God!"

Jesus said that in the world you will have tribulation (things that crush you), but be of good cheer, I have overcome the world. (John 16:33)

Another interesting thing about this verse is that He gives us a key to being able to choose joy.

"I have spoken unto you, that in me ye might have peace..."

Peace instead of fear; peace instead of anxiety; peace instead of turmoil; peace instead of hopelessness. This peace is only found "in Him". Choose joy – receive peace! The world considers peace as the absence of problems or trouble. The peace that Jesus gives is there regardless of your circumstances. Jesus said,

"Peace I give to you. It's not like the world's idea of peace, it's My peace."

Each time a shake-up happens there is great opportunity for God's will to prevail. To know God's will is to know what He wants to happen – His plan of action. He created you to be an overcomer. This is God's will. Maybe you haven't nailed down the meaning of overcomer. It' a military term suggesting combat against the enemy – to win after a hard struggle and to obtain victory. Jesus has overcome therefore, you can overcome. The realization of these important truths in our everyday life is certainly cause for great joy, celebration and dancing.

"...In the world you will have tribulation; but be of good cheer, I have overcome the world." John 16:33b

"Thanks be to God who gives us the victory through our Lord Jesus Christ."

1 Corinthians 15:57

CHAPTER 12

VICTORY OVER
THE ENEMY

There is no shortage of information in the Word of God concerning the enemy: God's enemy and every believer's enemy. One of the most revealing is found in Ephesians 6:12.

"For we wrestle not against flesh and blood, but against principalities, against powers, against the rulers of the darkness of this world, against spiritual wickedness in high places."

Satan has a kingdom. He is well organized and never lacks for loyal subjects to do his bidding. Perhaps you've heard, "Satan made me do it." In some small measure that may be true, but he's not near as powerful as he gets credit for. However, you can be sure he has fully qualified officers assigned to your case. That would be the fallen angels who are fighting with him; demonic spirits that prey on human weakness.

There is a secret the enemy does not want you to be aware of. The only thing he has to work with to accomplish his desire to steal, kill, and destroy, is what he finds in the heart of man — those human, often hidden desires inside each person. These may be hidden from those around us: family, friends, people at work, etc. They are not hidden from the enemy of our soul.

Here are three common heart issues where the enemy has an open door to set a trap and do his evil work in an individual. This is not a complete list, of course.

1. <u>Pleasure, passion or lust – Desires of the flesh</u>

This is enemy #1 – operating through the physical body as a result of the fallen, depraved nature. It is a propensity to do evil catering to appetites and impulses of the carnal nature. Jesus taught that evil things come from within the heart and defile a man. (Mark 7:23)

There are many temptations we must continue to watch for: It could be a contentious selfish nature that will rob you of peace; a spirit of arrogance that thinks more highly of yourself than you should; always comparing yourself to others; materialism that puts more emphasis on the physical world than on the things of God; lust for sexual pleasure outside of the will of God, etc. These kind of sin problems give Satan an opening to destroy the abundant life Jesus came to give. As we seek to grow each day the Holy Spirit will reveal things we need to repent of. To repent means to change your mind and turn away from sin and back to God, humbly acknowledging the sin against God. We have God's promise of forgiveness and cleansing. Our Father loves us too much to leave us as we are. The blood of Jesus continually cleanses us of sin as we repent. We are becoming more like Jesus each step of the way. As a believer the power of the flesh is broken. You do not have to be controlled by the enemy since you have been redeemed by the blood of Christ.

The enemy doesn't use new tactics. He has been using the same ones quite successfully for centuries and they continue to work on unsuspecting men and women. He started with tricking Eve in the Garden of Eden with lies and deception. Jesus called the devil a liar in John

8:44. Even though Eve had her needs being met she had a desire for human self-rule and a thirst for power. She doubted God. (We won't even mention Adam's problem.) Great was the fall!

An abnormal desire for more of this world's goods goes hand in hand with all kinds of fear: fear of not having enough; fear of not being good enough – not measuring up; fear of not making it. Just as faith comes by hearing the Word of God, fear comes by hearing the enemy's lies, entertaining negative thoughts, listening to garbage or junk.

Fear begins in the mind. Dwelling on negative reports; comparing yourself with other people's failure or success stories can be a major source of discontent, producing fear and anxiety. In the account of what happened in the Garden we soon find Adam and Eve hiding from God. (Gen.3:8)

In Philippians 4:8, Paul's advice for replacing anxiety lists truth first. This is one of the things the Spirit of God seems to be repeating today – truth matters! As you come before God with complete openness of heart and total transparency the purifying light of His Word becomes the solid certainty you can confidently stake your life upon. It's called the B-I-B-L-E! There is no other source for truth.

I wish I could say this is easy but we know it is not. We're at war against the enemy as well as our own fleshly desires. These are equally powerful and today many believers are being destroyed by failing to recognize what we are up against. It may help to take an inventory of your past mistakes. How did the enemy trick you into making such a disastrous mess? Chances are the same weakness still exists and the enemy is just waiting for another chance to continue his evil plan to make sure you do not live a victorious life in Christ.

Read 1 Peter 1:14-16 from The Passion Translation.

"As God's obedient children, never again shape your lives by the desires that you followed when you didn't know better. Instead, shape your lives to become like the Holy One who called you for Scripture says: You are to be holy, because I am holy."

2. <u>Pain or suffering</u>

This is such a delicate subject I almost left it out, but because it is so important I couldn't in good conscious. It would be wonderful to think the enemy has nothing to do with our physical problems. In fact, many actually believe this. The truth is the enemy is a bully. Yes, he will use anything he can to turn us away from God's love and care.

There are many different kinds of suffering that involve our total being: body, soul, and spirit. One principal applies to all: Jesus cares and He will always help you when you call on Him. Whether the current problem is sickness, disease, hardship, anxiety, loss, or unjust suffering, you can bring it to Jesus.

Recently in the midnight hour I began to question if the Father actually feels my pain. It was as though my mind was trying to reason it out. If He feels my personal pain then He must feel the pain of every person whether it is the deep sorrow of the death of a home; the frustration of dealing with impossible, seemingly unchangeable circumstances; the pain of facing an incurable disease; the loneliness after the departure of a loved one; the loss of your job; or the care of a sick child. Can God really care about every single one?

I began to think about the attributes of God that I believe to be true. He is all-powerful, all-knowing, and present everywhere. Yes, yes, and yes. But can He carry the personal pain for every person? Can I release these things into His hands? How can I know for sure?

Isaiah 53 immediately came into my mind. He has borne our grief and carried our sorrows… Here the Holy Spirit tells us that Jesus was the one who carried our sickness and endured the torment of our sufferings. Because he endured this punishment for us we are healed and made completely whole.

Psalm 103:2-4 is a great reminder of God's faithfulness to help in times of pain and suffering

"Bless the Lord, O my soul, and forget not all His benefits, Who forgives all your iniquities, Who heals all your diseases, Who redeems your life from destruction."

We find God's favor when we decide to please Him regardless the circumstances. Before seeking help elsewhere, run to Jesus. He is more than enough. His counsel is needed in order to make right decisions and choices in the midst of the storm. Philippians 4:6, 7 is a powerful word of encouragement for fellow sufferers.

"Be anxious for nothing, but in everything by prayer and supplication, with thanksgiving, let your requests be made known to God; and the peace of God, which surpasses all understanding, will guard your hearts and minds through Christ Jesus."

Here we are given the picture of a military soldier standing guard at your front door. God's power and peace stand guard as our protectors to give us victory over the enemy.

3. <u>Riches or power</u>

One of the clearest pictures of how the enemy gets involved in human weakness is found in the parable Jesus taught in Mark 4, on the heart condition of man. Four types of (soil) response to hearing the Word of God are given. Only one group has a teachable, hearing heart.

The third group listed is those who hear the word but "the cares of this world, the deceitfulness of riches, and the desires for other things choke the word..." In verse 15, Jesus explained, "Satan comes immediately and takes away the word..."

James 1:7 tells us how to have victory over the devil.

"Submit to God. Resist the devil and he will flee from you."

Submit to God

When you submit to God you come into agreement with God's Word and God's will for your life. You will reject the lies of the enemy and embrace what God says about the situation. Read Philippians 4:6, 7 again. These two scriptures explain how to submit to God – you talk to Him. Give all your worries into His capable hands.

Resist the devil

To resist the devil is to take your stand against him, forsaking your own bent toward sin, and fully embracing our Lord Jesus and His Word. When these two things are firmly in place: submitting to God and resisting the devil, no enemy can stand against you.

Remember, this has been made possible because of Jesus. He was fully submitted to God and He completely resisted the enemy. He won this victory for us. Today, in Christ we are victorious warriors. We are to look to Jesus, the author and finisher of our faith.

4. <u>Unforgiveness and Offense</u>

This has to be the most subtle form of destruction the enemy uses to do the most damage.

Offense

It's amazing how easy it is to become offended of the simplest thing. Someone gives you a strange look and you immediately think he is making fun of you. Friends are in a huddle talking and laughing and you were not included. You just know they left you out deliberately. Your friend was asked to step down from his position and even though you do not know why this happened you think it was unfair and want to get even. Your child's teacher did not choose him for the lead in the class play. These are offenses the enemy uses to distract us or to get us off the right path. Offenses can be real or even perceived hurt. Every believer must learn to recognize a temptation to be offended and immediately take it to Jesus in prayer.

You remember the old saying, Give him an inch and he will take a mile. That's what the enemy does when you allow offense to take root in your heart. There's no limit to the destruction that takes place. You will do things you would never have imagined possible.

Proverbs 18:19 "A brother offended is harder to be won than a strong city; and their contentions are like the bars of a castle."

Unforgiveness

Matthew 6:13, 14 "For if you forgive men their trespasses, your heavenly Father will also forgive you. But if you forgive not men their trespasses, neither will your Father forgive your trespasses."

When someone has hurt you and you cannot forgive him this becomes a very serious matter. God gets involved depending on how you handle the situation. Then the enemy also gets involved. When you refuse to forgive you allow unforgiveness to open the door to the enemy. You may carry this around with you for years and the longer you are bothered by it the deeper you are wounded. The other person is not affected at all, but you are the one being hurt.

What are you to do? It becomes very important to remember how much our Heavenly Father has forgiven you. Turn them over to Jesus. He is the one who can heal your broken spirit. Remember

King David wrote in Psalm 23, "He restores my soul."

Every time you choose to forgive or refuse to become offended you are resisting the devil and he loses another battle. You can have victory over the enemy!

"Thanks be to God who gives us the victory through our Lord Jesus Christ."

1 Corinthians 15:57

CHAPTER 13

VICTORY THROUGH LOVE

Love – such a simple four letter word, yet so misunderstood, misused, and often mistaken. There are several meanings for love in our English language, but only one will produce victory.

God is love.

Agape love comes from God who is love. This kind of love is as big as God, Himself. The word says, "God is love", not God has love or God gives love, but God is love. That's who God is. Everything we can know about God as revealed in God's Word points to divine love, freely given, unconditional, always working on our behalf for the highest good. The power of God's love is the basis for everything He does.

The facts we find throughout God's Word help us understand the love of God. However, I'm convinced we will never completely understand agape love. Every time I think I have finally wrapped my mind around this love the Holy Spirit reveals another dimension I have never considered before. This must be what Jeremiah 33:3 means. ." These are the days of great and mighty things for sure.

> *"Call to Me and I will answer you and show you great and mighty things which you do not know."*

When I think of God's love I like to begin with Jeremiah 31:3a

> *"...Yes, I have loved you with an everlasting love therefore with loving kindness I have drawn you."*

Only a God who is love could make such a promise. What a contrast between human love and divine love that will never end.

We have often misunderstood our Father in Heaven who is love by comparing Him with people we know. How do you picture God? An old grandfather figure that spoils His kids and overlooks any possible wrong in their lives? A stingy man who withholds good things? An angry, demanding slave owner looking for something to punish you for? An absentee dad you can never talk to? We must be careful about our perception of Almighty God and stick to what He has revealed about Himself in His Word. Of all God's attributes, love leads the way. God is love.

Every move of God has been saturated with divine love that never fails from Genesis 1:1 to Revelation 22:21, because God is love! If you can believe this it will change your life.

Think about this scene: Almighty God, Love Himself: Father, Son, and Holy Spirit met in the Counsel Room of Heaven before the foundation of the world and laid out a plan that cannot be changed. Love planned everything from beginning to end. There are no flaws in God's perfect plan. Human error cannot change it; no enemy from hell can stop it. Perhaps we have under-valued the might and power of Almighty God. He accomplishes everything He set out to do and even wrote it down so we could make no mistake about it. God is love!

There are those who might picture God as a frustrated leader who had to come up with Plan B or Plan C, when Plan A didn't work out. Nothing could be further from the truth. Nothing man has or has not done catches God off guard. His plan has everything factored in and our victory is secured.

And then, wonder of wonders, we may be guilty of thinking of God as a strong and loving man who was willing to sacrifice His only Son to populate heaven but has no desire or power to change lives today. Please do not misunderstand what I'm saying. I value my salvation and am completely confident in the knowledge I have a home being prepared for me where there will be no pain, sorrow, or sin – a place where God lives and every believer who has departed this life is with Him forever.

However, what I value most is the power of God who is living in me and who changed me completely. I was once in darkness and today I walk in the light; I was once controlled by a sin nature and now I have been delivered from satan's domain. This power is called Holy Spirit and He is also God, who is love. He is powerful enough to wash away the dry crusty remains of unbelief. (Borrowed from The Passion Translation).

1 Thessalonians 5:23, 24, is a prayer that will

surely be answered for every believer. Note in this precious promise that He will do it!

> *"Now may the God of peace Himself sanctify you completely; and may your whole spirit, soul, and body be preserved blameless at the coming of our Lord Jesus Christ. He who calls you is faithful, who also will do it."*

All through the New Testament we are encouraged to welcome the work of Holy Spirit in our lives. This operating power of God is vital to the life Jesus came to give – life more abundant. How can we ignore Him? He is the gift of God that rescues us from life's tragedies, failures, and fears. The work of Holy Spirit operates by love – always present, always patient, always available.

What does love look like?

One of the questions that come to mind when we consider the love of God has to be, what would a believer's life be like if God was not love?

In the first place, if God was not love there would be no salvation or deliverance from the power of sin and God's forgiveness along with complete wholeness. That's the true meaning behind the beloved scripture, John 3:16.

"For God so loved the world that He gave His only begotten Son that whosoever believes in Him will not perish but have everlasting life."

God so loved…that He gave. If God was not love would He have given His Son at all? 1 John 3:16 explains,

"By this we know love, because He laid down His life for us."

Without a God who is love there would be no peace – no joy. Actually, there would be no fruit of the Spirit. Of the nine given to us in Galatians 5:22, 23 love is listed first. These all depend on the power of love to be fully functional in a believer's life. This happens when you are born-again and the Holy Spirit of God comes to live inside, along with God's love. As you grow spiritually the fruit of the Spirit will begin to develop with visible results that can be clearly seen.

One of the most beautiful descriptions of God's love was penned by Frederick Lehman in 1917, in a hymn titled, The Love of God. This is the 3rd verse:

> Could we with ink the ocean fill and were the skies of parchment made; were every stalk on earth a quill and everyone a scribe by trade. To write the love of God above would drain the ocean dry. Nor could the scroll contain the whole, though stretched from sky to sky.

Love in action.

Growing up in the family of God we develop characteristics of our Lord – the greatest being love. Just before Jesus was crucified He began to prepare His disciples of His departure. John recorded this in John 13:34, 35.

"A new commandment I give to you that you love one another as I have loved you... by this all will know that you are My disciples..."

Jesus set forth a high standard for us, to love each other as much as He loved us. God's plan is for His children to show the world what He is like. In following Jesus we learn to love like He loves and in this way everyone will know we are His true followers.

Jesus' love is demonstrated through us in five categories:

GOD – Deuteronomy 6:5 "You shall love the Lord your God with all your heart, with all your soul, and with all your strength."

How can you love God with everything you are? Jesus answered this question in John 14:21 24 saying if you love Him you will obey His Word and if you do not keep His words you do not love Him.

NEIGHBORS – Matthew 22:39 "You shall love your neighbor as yourself."

YOURSELF – Ephesians 5:29 "For no one

ever hated his own flesh but nourishes and cherishes it…"

Those who think they do not love themselves are probably the ones who think of themselves more highly than they should. This is called pride, the exalting, pleasing and preserving of self and its desires.

When Jesus said, "love your neighbor as you love yourselves", He's not talking about an unhealthy, arrogant attitude of putting yourself first. Love for oneself is responding to the value and worth our Heavenly Father places on us. God put a high value on you when He gave His Son as a sacrifice.(John 3:16) He sees you in Christ, one of His own. If you have received Jesus you are the temple of the Holy Spirit who lives in you. (1 Cor. 6:19)

OTHERS – 1 John 4:7 "Let us love one another, for love is of God and everyone who loves is born of God and knows God."

We are taught to encourage one another, to build up each other, and to show hospitality among ourselves. This is the family of God and Jesus sent the Holy Spirit of God into our hearts to help us keep unity among ourselves.

ENEMIES – Matthew 5:44 "I say to you, love

your enemies, bless those who curse you, do good to those who hate you and pray for those who spitefully use you and persecute you."

There seems to be a distinction between loving others and loving our enemies. Others could be exclusively those in the body of Christ, other believers, while enemies are those in the unbelieving world.

The Apostle Paul's magnificent hymn of love in 1 Corinthians 13 is a description of the love of God and the love He brings into every believer's life. We would be wise to examine our life side by side with this revelation.

- Faith without love is useless.
- Self-sacrifice unless based on love produces nothing.
- Love always puts others first.
- Love seeks the good in all circumstances.
- Love rejoices in truth.
- Love produces patient endurance.
- Love never fails.
- Love is greater than faith and hope because love is eternal.

"Thanks be to God who gives us the victory through our Lord Jesus Christ."

1 Corinthians 15:57

CHAPTER 14

VICTORY THROUGH THE CHURCH

The word church is a New Testament word not found under the Old Covenant. Jesus calls it, "My church", in Matthew 16:18, saying "I will build My church". On this occasion Jesus was talking to His disciples concerning His true identity. Peter had the privilege of receiving the revelation of who Jesus is from the Father in heaven. He declared,

"You are the Christ, the Son of the living God."

Jesus explained that it would be upon this revelation that He is "the Christ, the Son of the Living God", that would be the foundation stone (bedrock) of His church, and the power of death (gates of Hades) can never claim victory over anyone who belongs to God. This is explained to us in 1 Peter 2:6, 7.

"Behold, I lay in Zion a chief cornerstone, elect, precious, and he who believes on Him will by no means be put to shame...the stone which the builders rejected has become the chief cornerstone..."

This is Jesus, the Rock upon which the church is built. Jesus told Peter he would be one of the little rocks (along with many others) on which he would use to build.

"I say to you that you are Peter (meaning little pebble)..."

The church, established after Jesus' death and resurrection and coming of the Holy Spirit is God's governing force on the earth. We are a body of people who are members of His body, saved by the blood of Jesus and commissioned to expand and build God's Kingdom by influencing those around us.

1 Peter 2:4, 5 help with our understanding.

"Coming to Him as to a living stone, rejected indeed by men, but chosen by God and precious, you also, as living stones, are being build up a spiritual house..."

Today, more than ever before we must believe God's Word. Jesus said,

"I will build My church."

From the human eye the organized church of today may appear to be weak and insignificant. Think again. Much of the work of Jesus' church is stealth — not seen by the casual observer. The church is people of God, you and me, victorious warriors walking in the Spirit, led by our Savior, triumphant and secure.

How is this possible? Jesus did not say my people will build the church, or even Peter will build the church. He did say, quite definitely, "I will build My church." That's how you can be certain the church is alive and well. Jesus is building His church one person at a time.

You may be thinking, I'm not a member of a

church. This may be true that you do not attend a place where the church meets, however one thing will always be true of anyone who loves the Lord Jesus, you will want to obey God's Word. Hebrews 10:25 instructs us not to forsake meeting together with other believers.

If you have been born-again by believing Jesus died to pay your sin penalty and have asked His forgiveness, receiving Him as your personal Savior from sin, you belong to His church. In order to live the life Jesus died to give you it is important to obey what He tells you in His Word, the Bible. Obedience to the Word of God is the clear mark of a person who knows God.

I had a revelation recently from a verse I had read many times but just couldn't wrap my head around what it means. Paul is teaching about marriage in Ephesians 5, saying a man shall leave his mother and father and be joined only to his wife and the two shall be one. He then says this is a great mystery: He is speaking concerning Christ and the church. (v.32) The Holy Spirit began moving in my thoughts. I began to thank God that He knows me as a person – just Him and me. I don't have to stand in line to talk to Him, or meet with Him only in a large gathering of believers. I can come into His presence any time, for any reason. I belong to Him and He belongs to me. The church Jesus is building is made up of all those who have chosen to put Him first and now we are accepted in the Beloved – each individual loved, protected, and provided for by our Heavenly Father. Guess what song just began to play out in my mind: Oh, how I love Jesus. Oh, how I love Jesus. Oh, how I love Jesus, because He first loved me.

Let's take a look at several statements found in the Bible concerning the church Jesus is building.

- The church is Christ's body, every believer a member. (Ephesians 5:30)
- Christ gave His life for His church. (Ephesians 5:25)
- Jesus is the head of the church. (Ephesians 5:23)
- Jesus has set His church apart and cleansed her by the word. (Ephesians 5:26)
- The church is nourished and cherished by the Lord. (Ephesians 5:29)
- She is a glorious church, holy, without flaw. (Ephesians 5:27)

The New Testament contains 27 books written to local churches to instruct followers of Jesus in the things of God. They are known as disciplines of the faith. Many stumble at this because our human nature does not want to be told what to do. God's truth is not a suggestion. However, an interesting coincidence is that everyone lives by his own personal set of rules and even teach his children accordingly.

When you have young children you soon understand the importance of rules. First of all, rules are designed to help your child to live a happy, peaceful life and to learn to get along with others. (Luke 1:79) You enforce rules because you love your children and want what is best for them.

For example, one of your rules may be "you shall not tell a lie". It is always disappointing when a child refuses to obey what you have set down as a family rule. It becomes extremely hard to build trust. Sooner or later a liar will get into trouble. As a parent you try to correct this before serious problems arise.

Does God use disciplines in a similar manner? Of course He does. God is a good father and any good father teaches his child right from wrong for his/her good. Just as a parent builds a family, Jesus is building the family of God, His church. However, there is a huge difference in this comparison. Jesus will not fail to have victory through His church.

The Word of God teaches us what pleases God as well as what is not right in His eyes. (See Galatians 5:19-21; Ephesians 4:25-32) In Galatians 5, we find 17 cravings of the self-life listed along with 9 evidences of the Spirit controlled life.

It is important to remind ourselves in obedience to 2 Corinthians 13:5 to examine ourselves as to whether we are truly in the faith. Why would I say this? The answer is simple. There will be many who think they are saved and when they stand before God He will say, "Depart from Me, I never knew you." This is life and death and you want to get it right today.

One of the big mistakes we have made is dwelling on the human, fleshly nature rather than seeing ourselves in Christ Jesus. Galatians 5:24,

"Those who are Christ's have crucified the flesh with its passions and desires."

We now live under control of the Holy Spirit. He alone can give you power to live for Jesus. He alone produces the character of Jesus in us.

Let's look briefly at the character of the church Jesus is building. In examining each of these we are reminded that when someone receives Christ as Savior the Holy Spirit removes the tendency to be irritating or to rub people the wrong way. I'm sure you can testify to this truth. These are evidence of the new birth and the indwelling Spirit. If they are missing that individual is not saved.

"…now if anyone does not have the Spirit of Christ he is not His." Romans 8:9 "For as many as are (continually) led by the Spirit of God, these are the sons of God." Romans 8:14

- LOVE – In the church agape love is demonstrated by the 8 other principles the body of Christ live by. As I have already mentioned, agape love always seeks the highest good of others.
- JOY – Joy is happiness that circumstances cannot change. It is heart-felt excitement

in knowing God loves you and He will never leave you.

- PEACE – The confidence you have because of God's abiding presence.
- LONGSUFFERING – Patient endurance in all kinds of circumstances.
- KINDNESS – Gentleness displayed in dealing with others.
- GOODNESS – The Holy Spirit gives both the desire and power to be generous in all acts of goodness to others.
- TRUTHFULNESS – Total transparency and openness before God that transfers into the words we speak.
- GENTLENESS – Even tempered, forgiving and helpful.
- SELF-CONTROL – A believer under discipline of Holy Spirit in every area of life.

In the book of Revelation we read of all believers around God's throne worshiping God. These will be from every tongue, tribe, and nation on the earth. When you picture this scene are you there? Your children? Your neighbors? This is the true church that Jesus is building today.

"Thanks be to God who gives us the victory through our Lord Jesus Christ."

1 Corinthians 15:57

Surrounded

Gloria Russell

BELIEVE
BEYOND
BASICS

GLORIA RUSSELL

Living in your
Fortified Place

Finding Protection
in a Troubled World

GLORIA RUSSELL

LEGACY

GLORIA RUSSELL